Mary's Prayers
and
Martha's Recipes

MARY'S PRAYERS
AND
MARTHA'S RECIPES

Tommy Tenney

Fresh Bread

An Imprint of

Destiny Image® Publishers, Inc.
P.O. Box 310
Shippensburg, PA 17257-0310

ISBN 0-7684-2059-8

For Worldwide Distribution
Printed in the U.S.A.

This book and all other Destiny Image, Revival Press, MercyPlace, Fresh Bread, Destiny Image Fiction, and Treasure House books are available at Christian bookstores and distributors worldwide.

For a U.S. bookstore nearest you, call **1-800-722-6774**.
For more information on foreign distributors, call **717-532-3040**.

Or reach us on the Internet:
www.destinyimage.com

CONTENTS

INTRODUCTION

In *Chasing God, Serving Man*, I sought to negotiate a peace treaty between the Marys and the Marthas in the Church. We look for a resting place so that there can be peace—a refuge that is both a place for caring worship of the Lord and comforting support for humanity. It is my hope that the whole Body of Christ will create a home where the Marys entertain His divinity and the Marthas host His humanity.

"God wants both Mary and Martha in the house....

"The key is for God's people to cross the dividing line of passion and compassion and meet Him at the convergence of the cross— the single point in time and space where passion for His presence and compassion for His highest creation meet" (*Chasing God, Serving Man*, 156).

I am a God chaser who is in passionate pursuit of God. This is the heart of my ministry, GodChasers.network. I have given my life to inspire and motivate the Body of Christ to increase the intensity of their spiritual pursuit. But I do believe that God's people should get their hands dirty in the service of men. I have used my base of ministry to network these dual passions of the Marys and the Marthas, creating a resting place for these two ministries.

In *Mary's Prayers, Martha's Recipes* we have created a resource book that will help the Body of Christ build that resting place. This is a "how to" book that will answer the many questions you have on pursuit and service. There are a lot of books on prayer in the market and many great *spiritual* cookbooks that promote our life in God. Unfortunately, there are precious few prayer and compassion books that can inspire us on one hand and give us practical steps on the other.

We must put our "passion" into motion. Like the old phrase goes, "this is where the rubber meets the road." In this book the practical merges with the inspirational. The end product is just what you need to get you on the highway towards the passionate chase and compassionate action.

I am so excited to present this carefully constructed resource book to you. It will accomplish both objectives. It will serve as spiritual food that will strengthen you on your journey. On the other hand, it will also provide a road map to equip you with directions to reach that special place of passionate pursuit of God and compassionate service of men.

Mary's Prayers, Martha's Recipes is a collection of carefully crafted recipes for both seasons in your life. To create this recipe I have asked my many friends to help me produce this practical and inspiring collection. It will be spiritual support for your contemplative praying and sensible solutions for your compassionate serving.

I have also introduced into this recipe compelling classic ingredients from the past, combining them with living contemporary components from the present.

Our spiritual journey is filled with ebbs and flows. We have all felt the pull of the heavenly tides drawing us out into the depths of sweet contemplation, passionate prayer, and spiritual union with our Lord. It is from that very place that we also feel the earthly tug, drawing us towards the shore of human deprivation, societal misery, and public destitution.

In fact, if the truth were known, there is a little Mary and a little Martha in all of us. There are seasons in our lives when we are tucked away in the secret place, giving ourselves to prayer and contemplation. At other times we come out of that secret closet of intimate prayer and passionate pursuit searching for recipes that will enable us to touch the "hurting ones" all around us.

Then He appointed twelve, that they might be with Him and that He might send them out to preach (Mark 3:14).

Introduction

As we see from this Scripture in the Gospel of Mark, it has always been the heart of our Master to draw His disciples into Himself—preparing them in the place of His presence so that He might eventually send them out into the world.

Following is a story shared with me by my friend, Billy Joe Daugherty; it gives us a real life example of how God uses Marys and Marthas.

In 1989 we began conducting monthly outreach crusades in the government projects of our city. Using tents and community centers, we faithfully ministered year after year to people of all ages through evangelistic services, medical care, food, and clothing.

As the needs of people increased, more and more came to us with every imaginable need. This growing influx of people revealed to us the pressing need to have an onsite outreach in this area, which would better position us to meet their needs.

In 1998, a newspaper article identified the area of Tulsa as having the highest crime rate. With my wife, Sharon and our two children, I drove out to that area and we began to pray that God would give us land for an outreach center that would turn the tide of violence and make this a place of peace. We wanted to see Jesus exalted in the middle of this neighborhood.

Within a few days two sisters named Mary Trotter and Martha Cobb contacted me. They informed me that their grandfather had left an 80-acre farm to them in the very location over which we had prayed, and that they had a desire to see the land used by the Lord as a community outreach. As we walked the property, we sensed in the Spirit that this was, indeed, special ground; there was a reason it had never been developed.

The Lord brought together a team in our church who started to research the land in courthouse records. We were told the land would never be rezoned for the purposes we desired; thus began the lengthy process of preparing the appropriate documentation needed to present a case for a *special exception*.

In November 1999, we appeared before the Tulsa County Commission, requesting a special exception to be made that the land might be used as an outreach facility. A pastor from our church presented our case with charts and explanations of the plans. One of the commissioners surprised us by saying, "If you had sent Sharon Daugherty to sing, this deal would already be over." At that point we knew God had gone before us!

We were soon granted the zoning we requested, which enabled us to begin the first phase of our dream.

Today we have almost 25,000 square feet that is comprised of the following: a medical area with a pharmacy, dental offices, clothing distribution area, computer center, gym, kitchen, and dining areas with a food distribution center. Outdoor areas for sports and recreational activities make possible make year-round outreach.

Mary and Martha gave what they had—they gave the farm. And because they did, on that land today worship and work, miracles and mentoring, praise and play are taking place year-round.

We must learn to work like Martha and worship like Mary. It is essential that we do not do one to the exclusion of the other. It takes the loving service of Martha and the adoring prayers of Mary to complete the full ministry of the Body of Christ in this world.

It is possible to remain in the abiding presence of our Lord while at the same time experiencing a pouring out from that secret place an abundance of generous acts of mercy. The desire of the Lord is that His people learn how to balance the height of intercessory prayer and contemplative adoration with the breadth of caring behavior and compassionate ministry to the house of man.

With this resource book you will have the full complement of recipes you need to fulfill both callings. It will show you how to get your hands dirty in the compassionate service of man, while leading you to the place where you will get calloused knees in passionate worship of our Lord.

Section I

MARY'S PRAYERS

"Jesus' first encounter as a human on earth began with a "No Vacancy" sign in Bethlehem, marking the beginning of His frustrating search for a welcome mat on earth. The truth is that He went from a borrowed womb to a borrowed tomb in search of a place to rest His head. The outrageous paradox of this picture is the fact that this was the Incognito Owner, the Divine Creator who was begging for enough hospitality to be born in the lowly realm of the created."

These words from page 1 of my book *Chasing God, Serving Man*, highlight the divine search for an intimate place on the earth where He can be at one with His people. In this section I will present to you a combination of intimate writings from the past that will provide fuel for your chase along with contemporary material that will be a road map for that chase.

Along the way I would like for you to pull off to a "rest stop" and participate in spiritual exercises and reflective questions that enable you to personally engage in the truths you are reading.

Chapter One

CLASSIC DEVOTIONAL THOUGHTS ON PRAYER AND SPIRITUAL PURSUIT

There have always been God chasers, and the heritage of the Church is rich with the writings and actions of those who have passionately pursued the Lord. Each generation has produced its own company of God chasers. Often they were not recognized in their day. Only in future generations were their works discovered for the rich treasures they are. The wondrous words of these passionate lovers can add to our own contemplative consideration of the richness of our life in God. Do not read these quickly. Allow them to soak deep into your spirit and soften the ground of your inner soul.

Amy Carmichael

Amy Carmichael was born December 16, 1867 in, Millisle, Northern Ireland, the oldest of three sisters and four brothers. She was raised in the Presbyterian church.

During her adolescence Amy showed signs of a great poetic gift. In 1885 she had a mystical experience that set the course of her spiritual pursuit.

Amy's passion for missions was ignited in 1887 when she heard China Inland Mission founder Hudson Taylor speak. Five years later, God's words "Go ye" were all the confirmation she needed to set her course for foreign lands. She was rejected by C.I.M. because of her frail health, but in 1893 she served the Japanese mission as "Keswick missionary," and in 1895 she departed for India. Miss Carmichael soon formed the evangelizing "Woman's Band" and took in her first woman "refugee."

In 1900 she moved to the infamous Dohnavur, where she eventually founded the "Dohnavur Fellowship." In 1903 Amy's *Things as They Are* was published, launching her career as a prolific writer. In 1916 she founded "Sisters of the Common Life," a spiritual support group.

Miss Carmichael was crippled by a fall in 1931; four years later, she became bedridden. She remained thus until her death on January 18, 1951, and was buried at her beloved Dohnavur.[1]

"DISTRACTIONS IN PRAYER"

Sometimes, when some distraction has called us off, we cannot even remember for what we were praying. "Sometimes I finde that I had forgot what I was about, but when I began to forget I cannot tell." These words were written nearly 200 years ago, but they might have been written by some of us yesterday. "I pray giddily and circularly, and returne againe and againe to that I have said before, and perceive not that I do so"...

Sometimes nothing helps so much as to turn from trying to pray, and instead, to read on the knees of the spirit some familiar passage from the Bible, for those words have a power in them to effect that of which they speak. Another sure way into peace is found in a literal obedience to Colossians 3:16. Turn a psalm or a hymn into prayer, read or repeat it aloud, for to speak to oneself deep down in one's heart, using words that one knows and loves, is often a wonderfully quickening thing to do, and nothing more quickly and gently leads one into the place of peace, where prayer is born....

Sometimes we cannot find words...do not be afraid of silence in your prayer time. It may be that you are meant to listen, not to speak. So wait before the Lord. Wait in stillness...And in that stillness, assurance will come to you...You will know that you are heard; you will know that your Lord ponders the voice of your humble desires; you will hear quiet words spoken to you yourself, perhaps to your grateful surprise and refreshment.[2]

REFLECTIONS AND RECIPES

1. Create your own classic. Take a hymn and write it so that its meaning quickens your own heart.
    Example:
    Amazing! Grace, how **sweeeet** the sound
    That **saved**—oh hallelujah!—a wretch like me, oh yeah! This grace is for ME!
    I once (thank God its over!) was L–O–S–T, lost—but NOW, yes, NOW I AM
    FOUND!!! (Phew)
    Was blind (can you imagine the handicap that was?) but now I see. And Lord, what I see is You. You! You with the glory that surrounds Your throne. You with the love that swells my heart. You, with the immeasurable, unsurpassing greatness that makes You the Almighty God.

2. Have you ever been distracted while in prayer? What kinds of things distract you? If upcoming or forgotten tasks make their way into your brain, have a "to do" sheet near your place of meditation. Jot yourself notes so that you won't have to try to remember. Position the Martha part of your life in order so that the Mary can find her way to the feet of Jesus.

3. How comfortable are you with silence in your prayer time? Is it easy for you to listen and not to speak? In the stillness, can you find the still small voice of the Lord? Are you experienced in "hanging out" in the presence of God so that this time loses its boredom and becomes a delight?

4. When was the last time God surprised you in your daily time with Him? In what way did He surprise you? Anticipate God's delight in your relationship by letting Him provide refreshment and joy in new and interesting ways. Remember, as Creator, His ideas to surprise you are infinite.

5. "What an incredible dichotomy! On one hand we say, 'O come, Holy Spirit. Come and manifest Your presence among us.' When He comes, we say, 'I hope You didn't plan on staying too long....' We fail to turn divine visitation into holy habitation because we don't value His presence" (*Chasing God, Serving Man*, 99). Have you ever felt this way? List 25 ways you value the presence of God. Speak these to the Lord with sincerity. Ask Him to validate each reason in your mind and heart. Ask

Him to help you turn the discipline of daily devotion into a delightful experience as He changes you from the inside out.

Phoebe Palmer

Phoebe Palmer was born in 1807 and died in 1874. She is considered to be "The Mother of the Holiness Movement." This movement began in 1835 with her Tuesday Meetings for the Promotion of Holiness, which continued for 39 years in New York City, where she lived with her physician husband. The success of Phoebe Palmer's informal meetings encouraged other women to conduct the same type of ministry, and dozens of them sprang up throughout North America.

In the fall of 1857, she and her husband traveled to Hamilton, Ontario. There they attracted crowds of several thousand people when an afternoon prayer meeting became a ten-day revival meeting during which four hundred people were converted to Christ. They experienced similar successes in New York City and in England, where they preached for four years to packed houses. It is estimated that within her lifetime, Phoebe Palmer brought over 25,000 people to faith in Christ.

Often our focus has been to affect people and by that impress God. By pursuing Christ, Phoebe affected people. Our primary ministry is to Him. To be holy and acceptable to Him is the ultimate call.[3]

Union with Christ is the goal of every God chaser. Palmer challenges us to respond to the heavenly call of Christ our Groom.

"MARRIED TO THEE"

Surrender that heart in perpetual keeping to Him, and by the infinite virtue there is even in the touch (Mark 6:56) of Jesus, the defilement of sin is taken away. Resting in His embrace, the hidden springs of the heart are so turned, that the tide of its affections flows out to Him, and *through* Him upon such objects only as His own compassionate heart would love and cherish. Thus alone can you be brought to love just what God loves; and by this

16

process only can you, in heart and action, be brought to fall in spontaneously with all His designs, so that your interests will all be united with the interests of the Redeemer's kingdom.

If you ever thus take Christ as the Bridegroom of your soul, the decisive hour must arrive for the consummation of that union. It has only been delayed for want of an entire acquiescence on your part. The Heavenly Bridegroom even *now* is waiting with glorious attendants from the upper world to hear your decision, to bring on the consummation, and to ratify and record on the pages of eternity the infinitely responsible act. He now presents the terms of the covenant, and invites you in His strength to lay hold upon it....

> "Oh, happy day that fix'd my choice
> On Thee, my Saviour and my God!
> Well may this glowing heart rejoice,
> And tell its raptures all abroad."[4]

REFLECTIONS AND RECIPES

1. Create your own classic. Write an acceptance speech to the Bridegroom's proposal. Include in it your acknowledgment of His love toward you. Declare that you receive the knowledge of His loyalty and commitment to you. Let Him know that you understand the full weight of His part of the covenant He offers, and vow to uphold your end of that covenant.

2. Phoebe Palmer tells us that we are to love just what God loves. This means that you love the things He loves even if it goes against your nature. It also means that you stop loving those things that God does not love. How can you find out what God loves? How can you grow to love just what God loves?

3. What are the terms of the covenant Christ offers as Bridegroom? (Refer to Revelation, chapters 2, 3 and 21.) What is our part of the covenant? What is His?

4. Create a comparison/contrast of how an earthly couple pursues their wedding covenant and how Christ and the Church pursue their heavenly covenant. Include the following: surrender of the heart, love in action daily, willful decisions to embrace the other's desires, mutual submission, affection, and faithful companionship.

5. "Just enjoy a holy honeymoon with Him. Devote yourself to the totally abandoned pursuit of God. At the moment you least expect it you may hear God's still, small voice whisper, 'Get ready. After you know what it means to have your hair catch on fire in the supercharged atmosphere of the upper room of worship, you will hear a gentle knock at the door'" (*Chasing God, Serving Man*, 82). What does a honeymoon with God look like? What experiences would this include? How can you prioritize this in your current schedule?

Hannah More

Born in 1745 in Bristol, England, Hannah More was to become a champion of the disenfranchised of the world. Instead of quiet domesticity, in obscurity, Hannah blazed a trail for women. As a powerful writer she earned a fortune which she used to set up a cottage industry that printed millions of moral tracts that were distributed around the world. She became friends with John Newton, the ex-slave trader, who became her mentor. She joined in with William Wilberforce in the battle against the slave trade.

She has the honor of making English ladies the foremost agent in the education of the poor. The intensity of her love for the Lord Jesus was reflected in a life given for His people.

What an example of balance: the hearts of Mary and Martha beating within the same bosom. Hannah More proves that you can be passionate about His presence and at the same time be a servant to fellow man. She earned credibility in two realms, so that both worlds would heed her invitations. If you build it *He* will come...and *they* will come to see Him.[5]

"RELIGION OF THE HEART"

God is the fountain from which all streams of goodness flow. He is the center from which all rays of blessedness shine. All our actions are, therefore, only good insofar as they have a reference to Him: the streams must revert to their Fountain, the rays must converge again to their Center.

If love for God is the governing principle, this powerful spring will actuate all the movements of the reasonable creature. The essence of religious faith does not so much consist in actions as in affections. Though right actions may be performed where there are not right affections, they are a mere carcass, utterly devoid of soul, and therefore, of virtue. On the other hand, genuine affections cannot substantially and truly exist without producing right actions. Let it never be forgotten that a devout inclination which does not have life and vigor enough to ripen into action when the occasion presents itself has no place in the account of real goodness....

What a model for our humble imitation is that divine Person who was clothed with our humanity! He dwelt among us so that the pattern might be rendered more engaging and conformity to it made more practicable. His life was one of unbroken, universal charity. He never forgot that we are compounded both of soul and body, and after teaching the multitude, He fed them. He repulsed none for being ignorant, was impatient with none for being dull, despised none for being loathed by the world, and He rejected none for being sinners. Our Lord encouraged those whose forgiveness others criticized; in healing sicknesses He converted souls; He gave bread and forgave injuries. Christians must seek to express their morning devotions in their actions through the day.

Do We Really Love God?

Our love to God arises out of our emptiness; God's love to us out of His fulness. Our impoverishment draws us to that power which can relieve and to that goodness which can bless us. His overflowing love delights to make us partakers of the bounties He graciously imparts. We can only be said to love God when we endeavour to glorify Him, when we desire a participation of His nature, when we study to imitate His perfections.

We are sometimes inclined to suspect the love of God to us, while we too little suspect our own lack of love to Him....When the heart is devoted to God, we do not need to be perpetually reminded of our obligations to obey Him. They present themselves spontaneously and we fulfill them readily. We think not so much of the service as of the One served. The motivation which suggests the work inspires the pleasure. The performance is the gratification, and the omission is both a pain to the conscience and wound to the affections....

Though we cannot be always thinking of God, we may be always employed in His service. There must be intervals of our communion with Him, but there must be not intermission of our attachment to Him.[6]

REFLECTIONS AND RECIPES

1. Create your own classic. Write your own parable of how God is the fountain from which all streams of goodness flow. Within the parable show different ways (streams) that goodness is spread and how the source can be cut off.

2. Why we do what we do is the crux of the matter. Good works are judged not by their impact or by the amount of sacrifice involved, but by the affection for God which they express. Reflect on some of your recent "good works." Were they motivated by your love for God, or was there some other motivation?

3. Because Jesus was perfect, we tend to see His model of holy living as unattainable for us. However, this was the "divine Person who was clothed with our humanity!" Asking ourselves "what would Jesus do?" is a good way to examine our behavior, but "who would Jesus be?" is even better. How did Jesus relate the Father to mankind in *everything* He did? How can we relate the same thing in what we do?

4. Hannah More points out that Christ "repulsed none for being ignorant, was impatient with none for being dull, despised none for being loathed by the world, and He rejected none for being sinners." Can you say the same for yourself? Take time to ask the Lord in which of these attributes you need to grow this very week to become more like Christ. Partner with the Holy Spirit to attain measurable growth. Remember this, too, is done through affection toward the Lord, not just through determination to be better.

5. "God is searching for the Mary in you, for the passionate worshiper who will worship Him in spirit and in truth. Yet He also considers it your *duty* to 'offer up your body as a living sacrifice' to Him (a duty that the Martha in you would quickly answer with a passionate 'Yes, Lord!')...Jesus Christ...asks that we keep our priorities and passions straight. How?...offer yourself as a vehicle to transport Divinity into the world of lost, hurting, and searching humanity. It is there, where

Divinity meets humanity in the place of hospitality, that you find your true self" (*Chasing God, Serving Man*, 76-77). Explain what this means in your own words. Do you feel your priorities and passions are "straight"? What changes might you make?

Hannah Smith

Hannah Smith is the author of the popular classic, *The Christian's Secret of a Happy Life*, which was published in 1875. Its spiritual secrets of walking with God have been a great source of spiritual strength to many generations of God chasers.

The search for God finds its greatest hope as we look within, deep into our spirit, where Christ lives. Smith gives us a series of clues for developing our inner life for receiving the "Divine Seed" and preparing our spirit for ultimate union with Christ.

"A Lesson in the Interior Life"

"ALTHOUGH the fig-tree shall not blossom, neither shall fruit be in the vines: the labor of the olive shall fail, and the field shall yield no meat; the flock shall be cut off from the fold, and there shall be no herd in the stall: YET I will rejoice in the Lord, I will joy in the God of my salvation."

There come times in many lives, when, like this bird in the winter, the soul finds itself bereft of every comfort both outward and inward; when all seems dark, and all seems wrong, even; when everything in which we have trusted seems to fail us; when the promises are apparently unfulfilled, and our prayers gain no response; when there seems nothing left to rest on in earth or Heaven. And it is at such times as these that the brave little bird with its message is needed. "Although" all is wrong everywhere, "yet" there is still one thing left to rejoice in, and that is God; the "God of our salvation," who changes not, but is the same good, loving, tender God yesterday, today, and forever. We can joy in Him always, whether we have anything else to rejoice in or not.

By rejoicing in Him, however, I do not mean rejoicing in ourselves, although I fear most people think this is really what is meant. It is their feelings or their revelations or their experiences

21

that constitute the groundwork of their joy, and if none of these are satisfactory, they see no possibility of joy at all.

But the lesson the Lord is trying to teach us all the time is the lesson of self-effacement. He commands us to look away from self and all self's experiences, to crucify self and count it dead, to cease to be interested in self, and to know nothing and be interested in nothing but God.

Call to the Higher Places

The reason for this is that God has destined us for a higher life than the self-life. That just as He has destined the caterpillar to become the butterfly, and therefore has appointed the caterpillar life to die, in order that the butterfly life may take its place, so He has appointed our self-life to die in order that the divine life may become ours instead. The caterpillar effaces itself in its grub form, that it may evolve or develop into its butterfly form. It dies that it may live. And just so must we.

Therefore, the one most essential thing in this stage of our existence must be the death to self and the resurrection to a life only in God. And it is for this reason that the lesson of joy in the Lord, and not in self, must be learned. Every advancing soul must come sooner or later to the place where it can trust God, the bare God, if I may be allowed the expression, simply and only because of what He is in Himself, and not because of His promises or His gifts. It must learn to have its joy in Him alone, and to rejoice in Him when all else in Heaven and earth shall seem to fail.

The only way in which this place can be reached I believe, is by the soul being compelled to face in its own experience the loss of all things both inward and outward. I do not mean necessarily that all one's friends must die, or all one's money be lost: but I do mean that the soul shall find itself, from either inward or outward causes, desolate, and bereft, and empty of all consolation. It must come to the end of everything that is not God; and must have nothing else left to rest on within or without. It must experience just what the prophet meant when he wrote that "Although."

It must wade through the slough, and fall off of the precipice, and be swamped by the ocean, and at last find in the midst of them, and at the bottom of them, and behind them, the present, living, loving, omnipotent God! And then, and not until then, will it understand the prophet's exulting shout of triumph, and be able to join it: "YET I will rejoice in the Lord; I will joy in the God of my salvation."

And then, also, and not until then, will it know the full meaning of the verse that follows: "The Lord God is my strength, and He will make my feet like hind's feet, and He will make me to walk upon mine high places."

The soul often walks on what seem high places, which are, however, largely self-evolved and emotional, and have but little of God in them; and in moments of loss and failure and darkness, these high places become precipices of failure. But the high places to which the Lord brings the soul that rejoices only in Him, can be touched by no darkness or loss, for their very foundations are laid in the midst of an utter loss and death of all that is not God.

Trusting the Promiser

If we want an unwavering experience, therefore, we can find it only in the Lord, apart from all else; apart from His gifts, apart from His blessings, apart from all that can change or be affected by the changing conditions of our earthly life.

The prayer which is answered today, may seem to be unanswered tomorrow; the promises once so gloriously fulfilled, may cease to be a reality to us; the spiritual blessing which was at one time such a joy, may be utterly lost; and nothing of all we once trusted to and rested on may be left us, but the hungry and longing memory of it all. But when all else is gone, God is still left. Nothing changes Him. He is the same yesterday, today, and forever, and in Him is no variableness, neither shadow of turning. And the soul that finds its joy in Him alone, can suffer no wavering.

It is grand to trust in the promises, but it is grander still to trust in the Promiser. The promises may be misunderstood or misapplied, and at the moment when we are leaning all our weight upon them, they may seem utterly to fail us. But no one ever trusted in the Promiser and was confounded.

The God who is behind His promises and is infinitely greater than His promises, can never fail us in any emergency, and the soul that is stayed on Him cannot know anything but perfect peace....

All of God's saints in all ages have done this. Job said, out of the depths of sorrow and trial which few can equal, "Though He slay me yet will I trust in Him."

David could say in the moment of his keenest anguish, "Yea, though I walk through the valley of the shadow of death," yet "I will fear no evil; for Thou art with me." And again he could say, "God is our refuge and strength, a very present help in trouble. Therefore, will not we fear, though the earth be removed, and though the mountains be carried into the midst of the sea; though the waters thereof roar and be troubled; though the mountains shake with the swelling thereof...God is in the midst of her; she shall not be moved; God shall help her, and that right early."

Paul could say in the midst of his sorrows, "We are troubled on every side, yet not distressed; we are perplexed, but not in despair; persecuted, but not forsaken; cast down, but not destroyed... for which cause we faint not; but though our outward man perish, yet the inward man is renewed day by day. For our light affliction, which is but for a moment, worketh for us a far more exceeding and eternal weight of glory; while we look, not at the things which are seen, but at the things which are not seen; for the things which are seen are temporal; but the things which are not seen are eternal"...

Three Regions of the Spiritual Life

A writer on the interior life says, in effect, that our spiritual pathway is divided into three regions, very different from one another, and yet each one a necessary stage in the onward progress. First, there is the region of beginnings, which is a time full of sensible joys and delights, of fervent aspirations, of emotional experiences, and of many secret manifestations of God. Then comes a vast extent of wilderness, full of temptation, and trial, and conflict, of the loss of sensible manifestations, of dryness, and of inward and outward darkness and distress. And then, finally, if this desert period is faithfully traversed, there comes on the further side of it a region of mountain heights of uninterrupted union and communion with God, of superhuman detachment from everything earthly, of infinite contentment with the Divine will, and of marvellous transformation into the image of Christ.

I Trust Him Now

"Though the rain may fall and the wind be blowing,
And cold and chill is the wintry blast;
Though the cloudier sky is still cloudier growing,
And the dead leaves tell that summer is passed;
Yet my face I hold to the stormy heaven,
My heart is as calm as a summer sea;
Glad to receive what my God hath given,
Whate'er it be.
When I feel the cold, I can say, "He sends it,"
And His wind blows blessing I surely know;
For I've never a want but that He attends it;
And my heart beats warm, though the winds may blow
The soft sweet summer was warm and glowing,
Bright were the blossoms on every bough;
I trusted Him when the roses were blowing,
I trust Him now.
Small were my faith should it weakly falter,
Now that the roses have ceased to blow;

25

Frail were the trust that now should alter,
Doubting His love when the storm-clouds grow.
If I trust Him once I must trust Him ever,
And His way is best, though I stand or fall,
Through wind or storm He will leave me never,
For He sends all."

The Life of Divine Union

Not long afterward I was present at a meeting where the leader opened with reading John 15, and the words, "Without me ye can do nothing," struck me with amazement. Hundreds of times before I had read those words, and had thought that I understood them thoroughly. But now it seemed almost as though they must have been newly inserted in the Bible, so ablaze were they with wondrous meaning.

"There it is," I said to myself, "Jesus himself said so, that apart from Him we have no real life of any kind, whether we call it temporal or spiritual, and that, therefore, all living or doing that is without Him is of such a nature that God, who sees into the realities of things, calls it 'nothing.'" And then the question forced itself upon me as to whether any soul really believed this statement to be true; or, if believing it theoretically, whether any one made it practical in their daily walk and life. And I saw, as in a flash almost, that the real secret of divine union lay quite as much in this practical aspect of it as in any interior revealings or experiences. For if I do nothing, literally nothing, apart from Christ, I am of course united to Him in a continual oneness that cannot be questioned or gainsaid; while if I live a large part of my daily life and perform a large part of my daily work apart from Him, I have no real union, no matter how exalted and delightful my emotions concerning it may be....

For I am very sure that the wide divorce made between things spiritual and things temporal, of which I have spoken, has done more than almost anything else to hinder a realized interior union with God, and to put all religion so outside of the pale of common life

26

as to make it an almost unattainable thing to the ordinary mass of mankind. Moreover it has introduced an unnatural constraint and stiltedness into the experience of Christians that seems to shut them out from much of the free, happy, childlike ease that belongs of right to the children of God.

I feel, therefore, that it is of vital importance for us to understand the truth of this matter.

Connected to the Vine

And the thought that makes it clearest to me is this, that the fact of our oneness with Christ contains the whole thing in a nutshell. If we are one with Him, then of course in the very nature of things we can do nothing without Him. For that which is one cannot act as being two. And if I therefore do anything without Christ, then I am not one with Him in that thing, and like a branch severed from the vine I am withered and worthless. It is as if the branch should recognize its connection with and dependence upon the vine for most of its growth, and fruit-bearing, and climbing, but should feel a capacity in itself to grow and climb over a certain fence or around the trunk of a certain tree, and should therefore sever its connection with the vine for this part of its living. Of course that which thus sought an independent life would wither and die in the very nature of things. And just so is it with us who are branches of Christ the true vine. No independent action, whether small or great, is possible to us without withering and death, any more than to the branch of the natural vine.

This will show us at once how fatal to the realized oneness with Christ, for which our souls hunger, is the divorce I have spoken of. We have all realized, more or less, that without Him we cannot live our religious life, but when it comes to living our so-called temporal life, to keeping house or transacting business, or making calls, or darning stockings, or sweeping a room, or trimming a bonnet, or entertaining company, who is there that even theoretically thinks such things as these are to be done for Christ, and can only be rightly done as we abide in Him and do them in His strength?

Acknowledge God in All Your Ways

But if it is Christ working in the Christian who is to lead the prayer-meeting, then, since Christ and the Christian are one, it must be also Christ working in and through the Christian who is to keep the house and make the bargain; and one duty is therefore in the very essence of things as religious as the other. It is the man that makes the action, not the action the man. And as much solemnity and sweetness will thus be brought into our everyday domestic and social affairs as into the so-called religious occasions of life, if we will only "acknowledge God in all our ways," and do whatever we do, even if it be only eating and drinking, to His glory.

If our religion is really our life, and not merely something extraneous tacked on to our life, it must necessarily go into everything in which we live; and no act, however human or natural it may be, can be taken out of its control and guidance.

If God is with us always, then He is just as much with us in our business times and our social times as in our religious times, and one moment is as solemn with His presence as another.

If it is a fact that in Him we "live and move and have our being," then it is also a fact, whether we know it or not, that without Him we cannot do anything. And facts are stubborn things, thank God, and do not alter for all our feelings.

In Psalm 127:1, 2, we have a very striking illustration of this truth. The Psalmist says, "Except the Lord build the house, they labor in vain that build it: except the Lord keep the city, the watchman waketh but in vain. It is vain for you to rise up early, to sit up late, to eat the bread of sorrows; for so He giveth His beloved sleep." The two things here spoken of as being done in vain, unless the Lord is in the doing of them, are purely secular things, so called; simple business matters on the human plane of life. And whatever spiritual lesson they were intended to teach gains its impressiveness only from this, that these statements concerning God's presence in temporal things were statements of patent and incontrovertible facts.

God Is Present in All

In truth the Bible is full of this fact, and the only wonder is how any believer in the Bible could have overlooked it. From the building of cities down to the numbering of the hairs of our head and the noting of a sparrow's fall, throughout the whole range of homely daily living, God is declared to be present and to be the mainspring of it all. Whatever we do, even if it be such a purely physical thing as eating and drinking, we are to do for Him and to His glory, and we are exhorted to so live and so walk in the light in everything, as to have it made manifest of our works, temporal as well as spiritual, that "they are wrought in God."

There is unspeakable comfort in this for every loving Christian heart, in that it turns all of life into a sacrament, and makes the kitchen, or the workshop, or the nursery, or the parlor, as sweet and solemn a place of service to the Lord, and as real a means of union with Him, as the prayer-meeting, or the mission board, or the charitable visitation....

An old spiritual writer says something to this effect, that in order to become a saint it is not always necessary to change our works, but only to put an interior purpose towards God in them all; that we must begin to do for His glory and in His strength that which before we did for self and in self's capacity; which means, after all, just what our Lord meant when He said, "Without me ye can do nothing"....

Scientific men are seeking to resolve all forces in nature into one primal force. Unity of origin is the present cry of science. Light, heat, sound are all said to be the products of one force differently applied, and that force is motion. All things, say the scientists, can be resolved back to this. Whether they are right or wrong I cannot say; but the Bible reveals to us one grand primal force which is behind motion itself, and that is God-force. God is at the source of everything, God is the origin of everything, God is the explanation of everything. Without Him was not anything made that was made, and without Him is not anything done that is done.

A Mystery Resolved

Surely, then, it is not the announcement of any mystery, but the simple statement of a simple fact, when our Lord says, "Without me ye can do nothing"....

If, then, thou wouldst know, beloved reader, the interior divine union realized in thy soul, begin from this very day to put it out- wardly in practice as I have suggested. Offer each moment of thy living and each act of thy doing to God, and say to Him continu- ally, "Lord, I am doing this in Thee and for Thy glory. Thou art my strength, and my wisdom, and my all-sufficient supply for every need. I depend only upon Thee." Refuse utterly to live for a single moment or to perform a single act apart from Him. Per- sist in this until it becomes the established habit of thy soul. And sooner or later thou shalt surely know the longings of thy soul satisfied in the abiding presence of Christ, thy indwelling Life.[7]

Thomas à Kempis

Thomas à Kempis was born in 1379 and died in 1471. In the Netherlands, he became an Augustinian priest. The great devo- tional work of his life was *The Imitation of Christ.*

Thomas found a "new devotion" in Deventer, which was the focus and center of a revival in the Low Countries of Germany in the fourteenth century of the same fervor as the primitive Chris- tians at Jerusalem and Antioch in the first century. He was part of a community called the "Brothers and Sisters of the Common Life." They took no vows, but lived a life of poverty, chastity, and obedience....Thomas à Kempis' favorite subjects were the mys- tery of our Redemption, and the love of Jesus Christ as shown in His words and works.

If the "fulness...indwells Christ," as he wrote, then we can create the same indwelling by the "Imitation of Christ."[8]

"LOVING JESUS" (TAKEN FROM *THE IMITATION OF CHRIST*)

BLESSED is he who appreciates what it is to love Jesus and who despises himself for the sake of Jesus. Give up all other love for His, since He wishes to be loved alone above all things.

Affection for creatures is deceitful and inconstant, but the love of Jesus is true and enduring. He who clings to a creature will fall with its frailty, but he who gives himself to Jesus will ever be strengthened.

Love Him, then; keep Him as a friend. He will not leave you as others do, or let you suffer lasting death. Sometime, whether you will or not, you will have to part with everything. Cling, therefore, to Jesus in life and death; trust yourself to the glory of Him who alone can help you when all others fail.

Your Beloved is such that He will not accept what belongs to another—He wants your heart for Himself alone, to be enthroned therein as King in His own right. If you but knew how to free yourself entirely from all creatures, Jesus would gladly dwell within you.

You will find, apart from Him, that nearly all the trust you place in men is a total loss. Therefore, neither confide in nor depend upon a wind-shaken reed, for "all flesh is grass" (Is. 15:2) and all its glory, like the flower of grass, will fade away.

You will quickly be deceived if you look only to the outward appearance of men, and you will often be disappointed if you seek comfort and gain in them. If, however, you seek Jesus in all things, you will surely find Him. Likewise, if you seek yourself, you will find yourself—to your own ruin. For the man who does not seek Jesus does himself much greater harm than the whole world and all his enemies could ever do.

The Intimate Friendship of Jesus

WHEN Jesus is near, all is well and nothing seems difficult. When He is absent, all is hard. When Jesus does not speak within, all other comfort is empty, but if He says only a word, it brings great consolation.

Did not Mary Magdalene rise at once from her weeping when Martha said to her: "The Master is come, and calleth for thee"? (Jn. 11:28) Happy is the hour when Jesus calls one from tears to joy of spirit.

How dry and hard you are without Jesus! How foolish and vain if you desire anything but Him! Is it not a greater loss than losing the whole world? For what, without Jesus, can the world give you? Life without Him is a relentless hell, but living with Him is a sweet paradise. If Jesus be with you, no enemy can harm you.

He who finds Jesus finds a rare treasure, indeed, a good above every good, whereas he who loses Him loses more than the whole world. The man who lives without Jesus is the poorest of the poor, whereas no one is so rich as the man who lives in His grace.

It is a great art to know how to converse with Jesus, and great wisdom to know how to keep Him. Be humble and peaceful, and Jesus will be with you. Be devout and calm, and He will remain with you. You may quickly drive Him away and lose His grace, if you turn back to the outside world. And, if you drive Him away and lose Him, to whom will you go and whom will you then seek as a friend? You cannot live well without a friend, and if Jesus be not your friend above all else, you will be very sad and desolate. Thus, you are acting foolishly if you trust or rejoice in any other. Choose the opposition of the whole world rather than offend Jesus. Of all those who are dear to you, let Him be your special love. Let all things be loved for the sake of Jesus, but Jesus for His own sake.

Jesus Christ must be loved alone with a special love for He alone, of all friends, is good and faithful. For Him and in Him you must love friends and foes alike, and pray to Him that all may know and love Him.

Never desire special praise or love, for that belongs to God alone Who has no equal. Never wish that anyone's affection be centered in you, nor let yourself be taken up with the love of anyone, but let Jesus be in you and in every good man. Be pure and free within, unentangled with any creature.

Discovering the Sweetness of the Lord

You must bring to God a clean and open heart if you wish to attend and see how sweet the Lord is. Truly you will never attain this happiness unless His grace prepares you and draws you on so that you may forsake all things to be united with Him alone.

When the grace of God comes to a man he can do all things, but when it leaves him he becomes poor and weak, abandoned, as it were, to affliction. Yet, in this condition he should not become dejected or despair. On the contrary, he should calmly await the will of God and bear whatever befalls him in praise of Jesus Christ, for after winter comes summer, after night, the day, and after the storm, a great calm.[9]

REFLECTIONS AND RECIPES

1. Create your own classic: "Jesus Is My Rare Treasure." You have discovered a treasure of immeasurable value. Just as an explorer opens a treasure chest of rare gems, you look upon the character of Jesus, each trait as a precious jewel for your life. Write about the jewels of Jesus' nature that you have discovered. Let the wealth of who He is surround your heart as you speak of the value of each aspect of His character.

2. Thomas à Kempis says, "When Jesus is near, all is well and nothing seems difficult." The disciples were near Jesus just before the feeding of the five thousand. Why did the situation seem difficult to them? What situations or relationships seem difficult to you right now? How do you need to bring Jesus near so they shrink in light of who He is?

3. How has the grace of God come to you so that you could do something that seemed impossible or improbable? Can you recall a time when God's grace left you and you became poor, weak, and abandoned to affliction? Were you able to calmly await the will of God, praising Jesus Christ for the summer ahead? Why or why not?

4. If special praise or love belongs to God alone, why do we crave praise and love so much? How might you find the center of your affection in God? How might you address the need for special praise and love in your own heart? How does the release of this need bring purity and freedom within?

5. "Mary's great gift was her single-minded devotion to the Master when he was in the house...As I noted in *God's Favorite House*: "The Bride of Christ has grown accustomed to living in the King's house **in His absence**. If she would return to the passion and hunger of her first love, she would never be so content unless the King Himself were present with her in the house..." (*Chasing God, Serving Man*, 32). Do you live "well" in the absence of the King? Do you find yourself content that He is not there? What needs to be stirred inside of you to allow His presence to so move you that you will not be content without it?

S.D. Gordon

Born in the 1800s, S.D. Gordon would become a prolific writer, know for his passion and insight into the "quiet life" inside the believer. His books on "Quiet Talks" have sold over a million copies. "E.W. Kenyon said that 'S.D. Gordon is a sporadic outburst of divine grace. His is unusual, as are all of God's rare tools...he is perfectly balanced in the Word and in the Spirit. He represents that rare but vanishing class of spiritually minded men of the last generation.'"[10]

In this article Gordon introduces us to a critical issue of prayer—listening. Too often we don't take time out to hear what the Father is saying. In fact, "listening in prayer" is a lost art that needs to be rediscovered. Gordon will help us in that discovery.

"THE LISTENING SIDE OF PRAYER"

In prayer the ear is an organ of first importance. It is of equal importance with the tongue, but must be named first. For the ear leads the way to the tongue. The child hears a word before it speaks it. Through the ear comes the use of the tongue. Where the faculties are normal the tongue is trained only through the ear. This is nature's method. The mind is moulded largely through the ear and the eye. It reveals itself, and asserts itself largely through the tongue. What the ear lets in, the mind works over, and the tongue gives out.

It is a striking fact that the men who have been mightiest in prayer have known God well. They have seemed peculiarly sensitive to Him, and to be overawed with the sense of His love and His greatness. There are three of the Old Testament characters who are particularly mentioned as being mighty in prayer. Jeremiah tells that when God spoke to him about the deep perversity of that nation He exclaimed, "Though Moses and Samuel stood before Me My heart could not be towards this people." When James wants an illustration of a man of prayer for the scattered Jews, he speaks of Elijah, and of one particular crisis in his life, the praying on Carmel's tip-top.

These three men are Israel's great men in the great crises of its history. Moses was the maker and moulder of the nation. Samuel was the patient teacher who introduced a new order of things in the national life. Elijah was the rugged leader when the national worship of Jehovah was about to be officially overthrown. These three men, the maker, the teacher, the emergency leader are singled out in the record as peculiarly men of prayer.

Now regarding these men it is most interesting to observe what *listeners* they were to God's voice. Their ears were trained early and trained long, until great acuteness and sensitiveness to God's voice was the result. Special pains seem to have been taken with the first man, the nation's greatest giant, and history's greatest jurist. There were two distinct stages in the training of his ears. First there were the forty years of solitude in the desert sands, alone with the sheep, and the stars, and—God. His ears were being trained by silence. The bustle and confusion of Egypt's busy life were being taken out of his ears. How silent are God's voices. How few men are strong enough to be able to endure silence. For in silence God is speaking to the inner ear.

> "Let us then labour for an inward stillness—
> An inward stillness and an inward healing;
> That perfect silence where the lips and heart
> Are still, and we no longer entertain

Our own imperfect thoughts and vain opinions
But God alone speaks in us, and we wait
In singleness of heart, that we may know
His will, and in the silence of our spirits,
That we may do His will, and do that only."

—Longfellow....

The first stage of Moses' prayer-training was wearing the noise of Egypt out of his ears so he could hear the quiet fine tones of God's voice. He who would become skilled in prayer must take a silence course in the University of Arabia. Then came the second stage. Forty years were followed by forty days, twice over, of listening to God's speaking voice up in the mount. Such an ear-course as that made a skilled famous intercessor....

Training of the Inner Ear

With us the training is of the *inner* ear. And its first training, after the early childhood stage is passed, must usually be through the eye. What God has spoken to others has been written down for us. We hear through our eyes. The eye opens the way to the inner ear. God spoke in His word. He is still speaking in it and through it. The whole thought here is to get to *know God*. He reveals Himself in the word that comes from His lips, and through His messengers' lips. He reveals Himself in His dealings with men. Every incident and experience of these pages is a mirror held up to God's face. In them we may come to see Him....

Prayer is the word commonly used for all intercourse with God. But it should be kept in mind that that word covers and includes three forms of intercourse. All prayer grows up through, and ever continues in three stages.

Communion, Petition and Intercession

The first form of prayer is *communion*....Communion is fellowship with God. Not request for some particular thing; not asking, but simply enjoying Himself, loving Him, thinking about Him, how beautiful, and intelligent, and strong, and loving and lovable he is; talking to Him without words. That is the truest worship, thinking how worthy He is of all the best we can possibly bring to Him, and infinitely more....Adoration, worship belong to this first phase of prayer. Communion is the basis of all prayer. It is the essential breath of the true Christian life. It concerns just two, God and myself, yourself. Its influence is directly subjective. *It affects me.*

The second form of prayer is *petition*....Petition is definite request of God for something I need. A man's whole life is utterly dependent upon the giving hand of God. Everything we need comes from Him. Our friendships, ability to make money, health, strength in temptation, and in sorrow, guidance in difficult circumstances, and in all of life's movements; help of all sorts, financial, bodily, mental, spiritual—all come from God, and necessitate a constant touch with Him. There needs to be a constant stream of petition going up, many times wordless prayer. And there will be a constant return stream of answer and supply coming down. The door between God and one's own self must be kept ever open. The knob to be turned is on our side....The whole life hinges upon this continual intercourse with our wondrous God....It is subjective in its influence: *its reach is within.*

The third form of prayer is *intercession*. True prayer never stops with petition for one's self. It reaches out for others. The very word intercession implies a reaching out for some one else. It is standing as a go-between, a mutual friend, between God and some one who is either out of touch with Him, or is needing special help....It is the outward drive of prayer....Communion and petition are upward and downward. Intercession rests upon these two as its foundation. Communion and petition store the life with the power of God; intercession lets it out on behalf of others....Intercession is the full-bloomed plant whose roots and strength lie back and down in the other two forms. It is the form of prayer that helps God in His great love-plan for winning the planet back to its true sphere.[11]

REFLECTIONS AND RECIPES

1. Create your own classic: "Knowing God Well." Write your own recommendation letter for God as if He were applying for the job of Almighty. Be sure your letter shows your personal relationship with God and not just job performance.

2. S.D. Gordon speaks of three Old Testament characters that were particularly mentioned as being mighty in prayer—Moses, Samuel, and Elijah. What does each of their prayers teach you, and how can you use these prayers to change the way you are praying for a specific need?

3. How are you as a listener to God's voice? How acute is your spiritual hearing? Is your sensitivity to His presence increasing? How is God's voice silent to you? Have you ever been trained by His silence? What noise needs to be removed from your ears so that you can hear the "quiet fine tones" of God's voice?

4. How does one keep the door between God and man ever open? If the knob is on our side of the door, what keeps us from turning and opening it? What issues do you currently see that prevent or try to prevent you from grabbing the knob to the door and opening it? Is it a matter of will or desire for you? Why?

5. "When we lack the discipline and discernment to prioritize Divine presence over human performance, we are refusing to release our earthly 'loot' to gain God's best...Sometimes we can get such sensory overload that we miss those moments of divine visitation or impartation...Hebrews 12:1, 'Let us fling aside every encumbrance,' (Weymouth's translation)" (*Chasing God, Serving Man*, 55-57).

ENDNOTES

1. www.heroesofhistory.com/page49.html

2. Amy Carmichael, *Thou Givest...They Gather* (Fort Washington, PA: Christian Literature Crusade, 1958), pp. 45-48. Used by permission. Reprinted as is.

3. Tommy Tenney, *God's Favorite House Journal* (Shippensburg, PA: Fresh Bread, 2000), p. 71.

4. From *Entire Devotion To God*, copyright ©1998 by Schmul Publishing Company, Salem, OH. Used by permission.

5. Tenney, p. 25.

6. Hannah More, *The Religion of the Heart* (Burlington, NJ: D. Allinson & Co., 1811), updated by Donald L. Milam Jr., pp. 27, 33, 85-86.

7. www.ccel.org/s/smith_hw/secret/secret.htm

8. Tenney, p. 79.

9. www.ccel.org/k/kempis/imitation2/htm/i.htm

10. www.posword.org/articles/gordsd/prayer00.shtml

11. S.D. Gordon, *Quiet Talks on Prayer* (New York: Fleming Revell, n.d.), pp. 159-164; 37-40. Reprinted as is.

Chapter Two

CONTEMPORARY PORTRAITS OF PRAYER AND SPIRITUAL PURSUIT

It is my intent to merge contemplative reflections with practical proposals so that together they will assist you in your own "chasing" after God. It is great to thoughtfully deliberate on the words of others but it is equally important to personally apply the truths you are discovering. In this chapter some of my friends will share basic insights and instructions for your private pursuit. I will introduce you to ministries that will further your pursuit coupled with very useful materials to enhance your journey. I couldn't think of a better person to start with than my own mother. Her passionate pursuit of the Lord has inspired my own pursuit, and her thoughts and insight will be a constructive support for the management of your spiritual journey.

Practical Insights for the Praying Saint

THETUS TENNEY

Personal Prayer Time

Our personal prayer time is the most important we will ever spend.

The quality of our life, relationships in our life, and our accomplishments will be largely influenced and determined by *Our personal relationship with God.*

Our prayer must be more than ritual. It must be real.

Our personal prayer time is the primary building block for all we can become and all we ever do for God.

It takes commitment and time to build a spiritual relationship.[1]

BE CREATIVE! If you get in a rut, DON'T STAY THERE!

Prayer is so awesome, spanning time and eternity! Why should we ever become entangled with routine, or limited by narrow focus and tunnel vision? Enjoy your time with God!

Preparing For Prayer

Proper preparation will enhance our time spent in prayer.

Consider The Place

A prayer bench
    a desk
        a comfortable chair
            or even your kitchen table.
A prayer room
    a church auditorium
        your study
            your porch
                or even your bedroom.
While you walk
    while you drive

These are just some of the places for prayer.

In fact, any location where prayer is needed can become a place of prayer...

churches
    hospitals
        schools
            high-crime districts
            in cities
particular neighborhoods
    places of special events
        government buildings
            parks
                city streets.

The Postures

Kneel

...Peter...kneeled down, and prayed... (Acts 9:40).

Sit

...Came a sound from heaven...and it filled all the house where they were sitting... (Acts 2:2).

Bow

Oh come, let us worship and bow down... (Psalm 95:6).

Stand

...and when ye stand praying... (Mark 11:24).

Walk

Arise, walk through the land...for I will give it to thee (Genesis 13:17).

Praying at Different Times

Our culture seems to demand shifting of daily schedules. The work day begins at greatly varying times for each of us. Our prayer time will reflect this.

Our prayer time may also be determined by the season of our life. Schedules vary greatly among young families, singles and the retired. We should adjust and adapt the priority of our prayer time to the demands of our current stage of life.

This is the day the Lord hath made. (Psalm 118:24).

Give the day to God.

Early will I seek thee. (Psalm 63:1).

Pray early for guidance and help.

Quietly listen to the voice of God before the rush of life.

Oh satisfy us early with thy mercy, that we may rejoice... (Psalm 90:14).

Recognize God's sovereignty, grace, and mercy for this day and give Him praise.

...we will give ourselves continually to prayer... (Acts 6:4).

Stay in a prayerful state of mind through all your daily activities.

Praying at slack times

• Sitting at a red light - pray for the people in the cars around you.

• Waiting in line - bless the place of business and all employed there.

• While driving - bless each neighborhood.

• On the job - pray to be a witness to your co-workers.

• When cleaning the house - cover each room and those who frequent them with prayer and protection....

Reasons and Benefits of Special Times in Prayer

• To develop a more intimate relationship with God - Extended time in prayer will enhance our relationship with God.

• To renew our perspective - Special time in prayer will help us see God's view. Our spiritual man will be strengthened; our mind will be renewed.

• For intercession - Praying for family, friends, neighbors, those in ministry at home and around the world, for cities, nations, and those who need the gospel will bring remarkable results.

• Humbling ourselves in repentance and submission - Brings purity of heart and lives.

• Special times of prayer provide a unique opportunity for personal inventory and evaluation. This is of particular value at times when making important decisions.

- Special prayer time will enable us to recognize opportunities and proceed with confidence, as we pursue God's purposes and plans for us.

Changing your position or even location (go for a walk) can help you stay focused during an extended time of prayer....[2]

Life Style Praying

Pray without ceasing (I Thessalonians 5:17).

What a challenge!

What a relief!

Who ever has time to pray without ceasing?

Anyone who will consciously make a choice to do so.

Most all of us have more to do than we can get done. Consequently, we discipline ourselves to a set time for our personal prayer and Bible study. Yet this seldom allows time enough to pray for everything we need and want to pray for.

Lifestyle praying is the solution!

It is a wonderful relief from feeling guilty for not having enough time to pray as much as we want to.

Lifestyle praying is truly *"praying without ceasing..."* Prayer should become a highly developed spiritual skill, not just a monologue of requests.

It should be two-way communication, true communion between you and God.[3]

Fasting

Fasting is not for Him [God] "to be" or "to do." He *is*; He has already *done* His part. Now it is left up to us. **Fasting empowers.** That **power** will enable us to better reach our communities and our families.

The chosen fast in Isaiah 58:6-14 gives us these purposes for fasting:

- To loose the bands of wickedness
- To undo the heavy burdens
- To free the oppressed
- To break every yoke
- To act compassionately toward the needy
- For health
- For cleansing
- For righteousness
- To enter into the glory of the Lord
- To hasten God's answer
- To live in light
- For continual guidance
- To repair breaches
- To restore paths

These purposes become benefits:

- Victories
- Deliverance from enemies
- Spiritual understanding
- Strengthens prayer
- Blessings
- Guidance
- Authority over satan
- Power for the supernatural
- Decision making[4]

Corporate Prayer

One of the notable benefits of corporate prayer is synergy. Synergy is a wonderful word which means whenever there is cooperation, the result of the efforts expended will be greater than the sum of what each could do separately. As many a surprised farmer has discovered, one horse can pull six tons of weight, but two horses harnessed together can pull not twelve, but thirty-two tons! The Old Testament equation is that one can chase a thousand, but two can put ten thousand to flight! The New Testament lifts the limits. If two agree on earth—*all heaven is behind them!...*

Prayer was the catalyst for the successful spreading of the Gospel in the early Church. Luke mentions or alludes to prayer more than thirty times in the twenty-eight chapters of the Book of Acts....

The potential of corporate prayer is as limitless as the power of prayer....

It is the **foundation** and the **force** of all spiritual enterprise.[5]

In the nineteenth century, George Mueller lived and provided for the children of his orphanage on the strength of his prayers. He was a man of prayer and the Word. After his death his personal journals revealed over 50,000 entries of answered prayer.

Once when asked the secret behind the dramatic results of his prayers he confided that for over sixty years he had never petitioned God without appropriate scriptures to match the request....

Prayer should become a highly developed spiritual skill....Intercession is my prayerful appeal for another; supplication is making my own requests known; meditation is listening to what God says to me....

Prayer is yearning and desire fed on hope and grounded in faith. Faith comes by the Word (Romans 10:17)....

The prayer of the upright is God's delight (Proverbs 15:8). He is delighted to communicate with me and receive my requests through the medium of prayer. As a loving father he longs to give good gifts to those who ask on the premise of His Word (Matthew 7:11, John 15:7).

In today's hurried pace, praying more may not be easy, but it is essential. The world's demands must never preempt the Word. Righteousness must have high rank. These are not demands to be met, they are powers to be experienced. The Word, prayer, righteousness, and the blood and the name of Jesus Christ are mine for the taking. What more do I need?[6]

Be Still

"Be still and know that I am God..." (Psalm 46:12).

In our activity-oriented world, it is important for us to learn the art of being still in God's presence. Prayer is communication with God. The most effective communication is a two-way exchange.

Talking to God is important. Listening to God is just as important. God seldom yells. He often speaks to us through His Word and through our minds as we are quiet in His presence or as we meditate.

The word *still* in Psalm 46:10, is the Hebrew word *raphah* and means "let go." Read the entire chapter carefully and meditatively. Note the permanence of God in the midst of turmoil - *"God is..."* in verse 1,5,7, and 11. It is important for us to frequently "be still" and "let go" of all the things that harass our minds and focus on the fact that He is....

"...In quietness and in confidence shall be your strength..." (Isaiah 30:15). In quiet stillness expect His divine mind to speak to your mind. Listen to your spirit as it fellowships with His Spirit. This is prayer. Too often we do all of the talking and then rush away before He has communicated with us. In stillness He can speak to your mind and spirit with direction, instruction, encouragement, inspiration, or whatever is needed.

"Be still and know..." is a neglected part of prayer. Of course we must talk to God to praise, exult, worship, petition, and interceed; but we must train ourselves to listen as He talks to us....

"Intercession is God's listening to you. Meditation is your listening to God."[7]

Pray for One Another

There are no singular pronouns in the model prayer given to us by Jesus recorded in Matthew 6:9-13 and Luke 11:1-4: *"Our father...*

give us...lead us...deliver us..." Prayer is a personal exercise but it must be a corporate enterprise....

Our prayers are to go far beyond the boundaries of our personal needs, desires, and concerns. James wrote *"Confess your faults one to another, and pray one for another..."* (James 5:16). Perhaps this is more fully expressed in Galatians 6:1,2: *"If a man be overtaken in a fault, ye which are spiritual, restore such an one in the spirit of meekness: considering thyself, lest thou also be tempted."*

We are to pray one for another as though we had the same need. "Fault" in these two scriptures literally means a "falling aside" or a "mishap." We are to share the trauma of our "mishaps." They are to be confidently guarded and carried with sincere intense prayer....

Praying for others is spiritually therapeutic. Job's severe situation was turned around when he prayed for his friends (Job 41:10). Before Luke 6:28 was written, Job's tender spirit led him to fulfill it: *"Bless them that curse you, and pray for them which despitefully use you."*

When the Apostle James wrote the admonition to *"...pray one for another..."* (James 5:16) he connected it with healing and effective availing prayer. There is a supernatural force in praying for one another.[8]

Transfigured by Prayer

The event we have come to know as the transfiguration is recorded in three of the Gospels: Matthew, chapter 17; Mark, chapter 9; Luke, chapter 8.

"...He took Peter and John and James, and went up into a mountain to pray. And as he prayed the fashion of his countenance was altered, and his raiment was white and glistening." (Luke 9:28 and 29). This was a preview of the glorified Christ as John again saw and described Him in Revelation 1:12-18. As Jesus prayed, the glory within became outwardly evident.

When we were filled with the Holy Spirit; the nature, power, and glory of God became resident within us. As we pray, the glory within can become outwardly evident. Much time spent in His presence and His Word will change us to reflect His image.

"But we all, with open face beholding as in a glass the glory of the Lord, are changed into the same image from glory to glory, even as by the Spirit of the Lord" (II Corinthians 3:18).

The Phillips translation of this scripture reads: *"We...reflect like mirrors the glory of the Lord. We are transfigured in every increasing splendor into his own image and the transformation comes from the Lord who is the Spirit"* (II Corinthians 3:18/Phillips).[9]

Prayer Warrior

There is a principle we must remember. Whenever we dare to put forth our hand in power, there is a spiritual sequence set in motion.

In Acts 3, a classic example of this spiritual sequence begins....The mighty power of God was manifested by the miraculous healing of the lame man.

The second event in the sequence was the backlash of the enemies of God... (Acts 4:2,3).

Thank God, it doesn't end there!

They understood Satan's "bluff" and scare tactics. All that was needed for Peter and John to set the third event of the sequence into motion was just enough time for them to get to another prayer meeting.

It seems Peter and John understood God's multiplication of power, as recorded in Deuteronomy 32:30, because they now prayed as a company. And there came a shaking, a filling, and an empowering that continued through the entire Acts of the Apostles. The sequence continues....

They continued in power stretching forth their hands to the despised Samaritans and to the dead Dorcas. About that time, Herod stretched forth his hand against the church. However, the angel of the Lord returned to raise up the imprisoned, sleeping Peter and send him back to another prayer meeting (Acts 12)....

The Spirit-filled life of the believer is not a vacation; it is war-fare. As such, there are times of prolonged attack. It is vital to keep the ultimate end in perspective.... You may be tired, discouraged and frustrated - but do not be deceived. Fight on in Jesus' name, with the Word, and by the Blood....

The "Egypts" and "deserts" in our life are only training grounds for us to prove that they that be for us are more than they that be against us. And He that is in us is greater than he that surrounds us. Joseph, Moses, and Jesus were all preserved in Egypt.[10]

Prayer—Thrust of the Battle

The church is an army - a militant, victorious army.
We are a soldiers - good soldiers of Jesus Christ.
Our leader is the Lord - strong and mighty!
The thrust of battle is prayer....
Prayer warriors have offensive weapons, not defensive....

Demolishing strongholds, hurling mountains into the sea, and storming the gates of hell are not defensive actions (Matthew 17:20; 16:18). They are offensive tactics. The only rescue mission the church and its warriors are to engage in is the offensive action of rescuing souls held by the enemy.

We are not an army of weaklings. We are "*...endued with power from on high*" (Luke 24:49)....Our weapon is the Word of God....

The thrust of the battle is prayer. The energy for the battle is praise... (II Cor. 20:22)....

- Prayer connects me to this awesome power of mighty God.

- Prayer is the most incredible power ever given to man.

- Prayer has no restrictions or barriers.

- Prayer can accomplish the work of the Spirit next door or around the globe.

- Through prayer we can become a part of any ministry or work of the Spirit anywhere in this world. Through prayer we can help anybody anywhere.

- Prayer mixed with faith can defeat the enemy, change world events, find the lost, heal the sick, lift up the fallen, loose the hold of evil spirits, find guidance, enlist the help of angels, and more.

- Prayer can bless one man or a multitude.

- Prayer can open effectual doors. It can bring revival to a church or to a country.

- Prayer can tap into promises, provision, and power.

- Prayer knows no status restrictions. They youngest, the oldest, the poorest, the richest, the illiterate, and the educated all have equal access to God and his power through prayer.

- Prayer is as simple and direct as "Our Father."

- The Holy Spirit assists us in prayer... (Rom. 8:26).

- Prayer coupled with the weapon of the Word is the force of power for warfare.[11]

Activating Your Potential for Ministry

WAGNER LEADERSHIP INSTITUTE

When discussing appropriate contemporary ministries of compassion, it is necessary to answer the question of appropriate training: are the institutions of the day preparing men and women to exercise a true Martha servant-spirit while binding them to the Source through the Mary devotion? C. Peter Wagner has developed a school that addresses this preparation. It's mission includes equipping leaders in the necessary skills for effective ministry in the New Apostolic Reformation.

The Need

Most pastors agree that they were inadequately trained for the job of leading the local church. There is little doubt that churches are in desperate need of effectual leadership as the challenges confronting the church become more complex, more numerous, and more daunting.

The Question

How will those leaders be identified, developed and nurtured for effective ministry leadership? Is there an institution that is forward-looking and assumes the ideal role of reshaping candidates for revolutionary ministry?

The Educational Paradigm

The Wagner Institute transcends the traditional classroom format and incorporates a variety of learning events and experiences which rely more on impartation that on information. Furthermore, ministry in the Spirit receives equal emphasis to ministry in the Word and truth. This paradigm follows the blueprint of C. Peter Wagner, whose books on church growth and leadership are contemporary classics.

A Working Example: LifeWorks Twenty-Four/Seven

LifeWorks is a series of seminars providing biblical solutions to the challenges of implementing kingdom principles is the marketplace of the 21st century. Whether the Christian is a manager or employee, this course takes an in depth look at the prophetic and practical implications for life and business in the years immediately preceding the return of Jesus Christ. LifeWorks equips men and women to be as those of Issachar, who understand the times they are living in and what God's directives are to His people in the workplace.

Wagner Leadership Institute has working relationships with similar schools who are considered "affiliate institutions." In order to bring the location of classroom courses as near to the students as possible, WLI is establishing regional extension centers. It is the goal of WLI to have fully operational branches in 50 different nations of the world, keeping the program contextualized with each particular culture.[12]

Bringing the Word to Life Through Worship and the Arts

FRIENDS OF THE BRIDEGROOM

One may think that those who participate in arts ministries are part and parcel of Mary's devotion. However, the activity of the art form in its rehearsal and performance can protrude into more of a Martha service. Friends of the Bridegroom address this issue as they pursue a course to raise up worshipers of the Living God.

Their mission is carefully chosen: Through worship, prayer, intercession, and teaching, it is our desire to lead God's sons and daughters into a deeper intimacy and freedom in Jesus. We offer completely original worship CDs with fresh new music from the throne and prophetic artwork. We also offer worship meetings, and teachings, to enhance your daily worship experience.

The name of this ministry comes from John 3:29, "He that hath the bride is the Bridegroom: but, the friend of the Bridegroom, which standeth and heareth Him, rejoiceth greatly, because of the Bridegroom's voice: this my joy therefore is fulfilled."

Stephen and Lisa Swanson, directors of Friends of the Bridegroom, respond to this scripture, "In humility, in reverence, we serve an awesome God. Our desire is to empower and train His worshipers to live in the intimate embrace of our heavenly Bridegroom./ Our calling, through Jesus, is to release His 'friends,' His 'beloved,' to discover their gifts in worship, for the advancing of the Kingdom of God, and the preparation of the bride of Christ."

Friends of the Bridegroom offer workshops in dance, the song of the Lord, keyboard, David's tabernacle, scriptural foundations for worship and "harp and bowl" worship. One unique workshop is called "The Living Word." In which an illustrated sermon about the "Potter's Vessels" is portrayed with music, scripture, exhortation, and a sculptor with clay on a potter's wheel.

An exciting part of the ministry is the Worship Camp for children. It is a week-long experience to "Rebuild the Tabernacle" of

David. Children study David's psalms and learn about worship. They combine worship and intercession, writing their own prayers, worship hymns and prophetic songs. Children also participate in various activities, including worship arts (crafts that portray the focus of the week), dance, David's Café (snacks with a message), and corporate gatherings of worship.

As this ministry crosses generations, it is setting forth a pattern of worship that will continue in the decades to follow. True devotion, pure worship, and art that gives God glory are manifested by those who have touched Friends of the Bridegroom.[13]

Equipping the Body of Christ for the Purpose of Prayer

INTERCESSORS INTERNATIONAL

Intercessors International is a ministry committed to teach, train and mobilize the body of Christ worldwide in the principles of prayer for the purpose of enhancing spiritual growth as well as furthering world evangelization; and to strengthen Christian leaders through prayer, encouragement and restoration.

Founded by Floyd and Elizabeth (Beth) Alves in 1972, the ministry was originally known as Alves Christian Outreach. In 1990 the name was changed to Intercessors International. The ministry focus has consistently been to equip others to pray more effectively and to bring and share the good news of the Gospel to the unreached.

The work of Intercessors International is broad, far-reaching and multi-faceted. Each outreach and program has a single common denominator: prayer. The number of intercessors who are trained and certified to teach Prayer Seminars around the world is ever-increasing.

There is opportunity to join teams on prayer journeys to many Asian, Middle East and Third World nations. Another facet of this ministry offers 24-hour, on-site prayer coverage for national and international events.

Intercessors International's corporate office is in Bulverde, Texas. Other offices are located in Arlington, Texas; Colorado Springs, Colorado; Austin, Texas; Tulsa, Oklahoma; the Netherlands; and an Asian office in Korea.

Following are some of the types of services of Intercessors International.

The Watchman and The Warrior: A Prayer Shield for Leaders

This facet of the ministry provides daily prayer support for ministers, missionaries and spiritual leaders in the Body of Christ. Those enlisted in the Prayer Shield program must be certified through an Intercessors International prayer seminar and commit to minimum of one year participation in the prayer shield for leaders.

Prayer Seminars

A Prayer Seminar is an intensive 18-hour teaching experience that trains Christians to intercede for ministers, missionaries and spiritual leaders worldwide. Participants also learn to unleash the power of prayer in their own lives as they intercede for families, churches and communities.

The President's PIT Crew

* The role of a pit crew for a race car driver is to see that every need of the driver and the car which he has entered into the race is met. In the same way, we undergird the President through a weekly prayer initiative based on scripture. The job of the President's PIT Crew is to pray regularly for the personal needs of the President of the United States, his family, and the Secret Service agents who guard him. Personal does not mean that the ministry has personal contact with the President, but that prayer is made for matters that concern the President personally.

Ministry to and for the Local Church

With a trained Intercessors International leader at its head, a team of intercessors from within the church or ministry is recruited and trained in the principles of prayer. A program of prayer, customized to address the needs of the church or ministry, is put in place as we launch, guide and supervise the program.

There are special seminars where teaching is offered to help train members within the local churches to undergird their own pastors and ministries of prayer.

Prayer Force

Intercessors International works in conjunction with the World Prayer Center's Prayer Force encouraging churches to become prayer based and providing them with prayer training to: raise up a Prayer Leader, form a Prayer Shield and train intercessors. Segments of the Prayer Seminar will be compiled with NALCPL (National Association of Local Church Prayer Leaders) teachings in video and satellite programs. The satellite program is scheduled to begin in the fall of 2002 and held monthly with a 90 minute training.

Ministry for Prisoners

These eight-hour Prayer Training Seminars are held within the walls of state and federal prisons. In conjunction with the seminar, books and other ministry materials on prayer are donated to each prison library. In addition, each attending prisoner receives a copy of The Mighty Warrior book and workbook.

This is a scholarship program.

On-Site Prayer Coverage for Conferences and Special Events

Since 1993, Intercessors International has provided 24-hour on-site prayer coverage for national and international conferences and special events. Examples include Teenage Congress, Get Ready Conferences and the March for Jesus in Germany; the In Your Presence Conference in Holland, Get Ready Conferences in Mongolia and Switzerland, EXPLO Conferences in Switzerland for Campus Crusade for Christ, Victory Word Explosion in Oklahoma and the Passion in Texas conference.

Beginning 3-6 months prior to the event and involving the training of 80 to 120 local intercessors, this valuable service brings 12-15 experienced intercessors to a conference to teach, train, lead and pray. Many miracles have taken place and one imminent danger was diverted as a direct result of the intercessors prayer of these teams.[14]

Binding God's People Together in Prayer

INTERCESSORS FOR AMERICA

Intercessors for America is a Christian ministry founded in 1973 which serves the Church of Jesus Christ by encouraging effective prayer and fasting for the Church, our nation, and their leaders. To that end we:

- Glorify Jesus Christ, seek to edify the Church and extend God's kingdom on earth;

- Maintain a serving posture toward the local church and its leaders; Cooperate with and complement other prayer ministries and like-minded organizations;

- Speak prophetically—sound the trumpet—concerning biblical moral issues;

- Adhere to biblical principles and godly conduct in all that we do;

- Carefully steward the resources entrusted to us;

- Stay modest in regards to structure, facilities and programs.

Mission: To fervently and humbly seek the supremacy of Jesus Christ in America through prevailing prayer and fasting. walking out the vision of America's Christian founders...

"I have often said it would be a thing very desirable, and very likely to be followed with a great blessing, if there could be some contrivance, that there should be an agreement of all God's people in America...to keep a Day of Fasting and Prayer to God; herein, we should all unite on the same day...It seems to me, it would mightily encourage and animate God's saints, in humbly and earnestly seeking God, for such blessings which concerns them all; and that it would be much for the rejoicing of all, to think, that at the same time such multitudes of God's dear children, far and near, were sending up their cries to the same common Father for the same motives."

-Jonathan Edwards, 1742

John D. Beckett helped found Intercessors for America in 1973 and serves as Chairman of the Board. John became President of the R.W. Beckett Corporation of Elyria, Ohio, in 1965 upon the death of his father, and subsequently built the business to worldwide leadership in the manufacture of residential and commercial oil burners. The company has acquired additional products. Mr. Beckett now serves as Chairman and CEO and oversees a new Beckett Advanced Technology Center. Mr. Beckett serves on the Board of Concerts of Prayer International, has been a member of America's National Prayer Committee. He serves on various other boards and councils.

Gary Bergel serves as President of Intercessors for America. Mr. Bergel has worked with IFA in various capacities since its founding in 1973. In 1985 the IFA national offices were moved to the Washington, DC area and he became Executive Director. He was named President in 1988. Gary serves at the executive level on the Board of America's National Prayer Committee, chairs the Prayer Committee of Operation Starting Line, is a member of the National Committee of Mission America, the Editorial Advisory Board for the *Pray!* Magazine, and works with many leaders in the U.S. and abroad.[14]

REFLECTIONS AND RECIPES

Warning: Spiritual Enzymes at Work

Americans desire quality…in the food they eat, the clothes they wear, the services they receive, etc. We can have the highest quality food, but unless our body releases the enzymes that break down that food for its proper use, we have partaken of those calories in vain. The quality of our spiritual life is directly proportional to our relationship with God. He releases the spiritual enzymes necessary for our relationships and accomplishments to fulfill His intended purpose. This chapter begins with spiritual enzymes from a praying mom and ends with four hands-on ministries that "jump start" the "enzyme rush."

1.   Create your own classic: "Transfigured by Prayer." Thetus Tenney believes that "as we pray, the glory within can become outwardly evident." Choose a week to be your week of prayer. Be sure all the events of your week (even time with family and sleeping) are dutifully written on your calendar. In every blank spot, make an appointment with "Prayer." Determine the number of hours you will pray that week. Now be prepared with a journal and a pen. Following your week of prayer, watch carefully to see whether other people look at you differently than before. Your attitude, your countenance, your body posture, your initiative; all should be different to some degree.

2.   "Be still and know that I am God" (Ps. 46:12). Picture yourself in the throne room of the Most High God. Place yourself before Him and peer into His face. Let yourself remain in His presence, basking in His glory as you would the sunshine, listening intently to His voice, as you would a gifted advisor. You don't need to even record the event. Just listen...and be still...and know...

3.   What is your potential for ministry? How do you activate it? If you were to write a training program for yourself, what spiritual discipline training would it include? Just as the Wagner Leadership Institute is "forward-looking," look to your future. If you don't prepare, you won't be ready to assume the post God has assigned you. What formal training might you need in a skill set? Take some time to pray over the future God has for you and what strategic plan you need to meet the challenge ahead.

4.   "Harp and bowl" ministry combines worship and intercession. As you read the descriptions of the ministries Friends of the Bridegroom, Intercessors International, and Intercessors for America, what rang true in your spirit to make you want to know more or participate in any of these? Let the Holy Spirit speak to your personal "harp and bowl" ministry, but also let Him challenge you in your participation in the Body of Christ.

5.   "All four Gospel accounts say the Holy Spirit is 'like a dove.' If you could picture people in the church carrying a dove, you would see some people carrying it with an open palm and allowing the dove to perch where and when he chooses. Many of them, though, would revert to their usual practice in life and enclose the dove in their tight fists to 'hold on to it.' This describes how many of us try to 'carry' the Holy Spirit. We want to 'hold onto' God with such a grip that we grieve

and quench the Holy Spirit in the process" (*Chasing God, Serving Man*, 102-103). Which of the two pictures given most describes you and why? How are you going to entertain or host the Holy Spirit in your prayer life, in your worship, and in your intercessory prayer so that His mark will be on everything you do?

ENDNOTES

1. Teri Spears and Thetus Tenney, *First of All Prayer* (Tioga, LA: Focused Light Publications, 1997), p. 3. Used by permission. Reprinted as is.

2. Spears and Tenney, pp. 4-12.

3. Ibid., pp. 35-37.

4. Ibid., pp. 41-46.

5. Ibid., pp. 51-57.

6. Thetus Tenney, *Focused Light, Volume One* (Tioga, LA: Focused Light Publications, 1994), pp. 33-34. Used by permission. Reprinted as is.

7. Tenney, pp. 35-36.

8. Ibid., pp. 44-45.

9. Ibid., p. 46.

10. Thetus Tenney, *Focused Light, Volume Two* (Tioga, LA: Focused Light Publications, 1994), pp. 9-11. Used by permission. Reprinted as is.

11. Tenney, pp. 13-15.

12. www.wagnerleadership.org Used by permission. Reprinted as is.

13. www.fobworshipmin.org Used by permission. Reprinted as is.

14. www.intercessorsinternational.org Used by permission. Reprinted as is.

15. www.ifa-usapray.org and www.yifa.org Used by permission. Reprinted as is.

Section II

MARTHA'S RECIPES

"I've devoted most of my energies over the past few years to creating hunger for God's presence in the Church, but I am painfully aware that we will fail if our increased *passion* for God does not produce increased *compassion* for man....

"Until the Church comes to the place where divine passion and human compassion meet, there will be a credibility erosion. Nothing is accomplished when we merely point out the problem without providing solutions" (*Chasing God, Serving Man*, 136).

I have a lot of friends who are engaged in providing those solutions. Before I introduce you to them I have compiled some reflective writings that will help clarify the issues that we are dealing with. Before you can recommend a solution you must first recognize the problem.

These issues are not unique to our generation. Every generation has struggled with the challenges of balancing *passion* with *compassion*. These words reflect the struggle and will assist us in maintaining that balance.

Chapter Three

Classic Devotional Thoughts for Compassionate Action

To Preach Good Tidings unto the Meek:

To Bind up the Broken-hearted:

To proclaim Liberty to the Captives and the Opening of the Prison to Them that are Bound:

To Proclaim the Acceptable Year of the Lord, and the Day of Vengeance of our God:

To Comfort all that Mourn:

To Appoint unto them that Mourn in Zion:

To Give unto them—

Beauty for Ashes,

The Oil of Joy for Mourning,

The Garment of Praise for the Spirit of Heaviness.[1]

Henry Drummond

Henry Drummond (1851-1897), a professor at Edinburgh University in Scotland, had an inherent love for and broadly developed interests in natural science and religion. He strove to convey to others those glimpses of a wider outlook and flashes from a penetrating insight that had cheered and illuminated his own solitary path.

Of all the books that have been written about love, perhaps none have been as influential and inspirational as *The Greatest Thing in the World*. Based on the thirteenth chapter of First Corinthians, this classic message has directed millions of people to the way of true happiness. The simple beauty and positive truths of this dynamic sermon will encourage readers to practice the power and blessing of God's supreme gift to mankind: love.

I first received a copy of this little book when I was 16 years old. Its words impacted me so much that today I can still quote from Henry Drummond.[2]

"HIS SERVANTS SHALL SERVE"

"WHAT does God do all day?" once asked a little boy. One could wish that more grown-up people would ask so very real a question. Unfortunately, most of us are not even boys in religious intelligence, but only very unthinking children. It no more occurs to us that God is engaged in any particular work in the world than it occurs to a little child that its father does anything except be its father. Its father may be a Cabinet Minister absorbed in the nation's work, or an inventor deep in schemes for the world's good; but to this master-egoist he is father, and nothing more. Childhood, whether in the physical or moral world, is the great self-centred period of life; and a personal God who satisfies personal ends is all that for a long time many a Christian understands.

But as clearly as there comes to the growing child a knowledge of its father's part in the world, and a sense of what real life means, there must come to every Christian whose growth is true some richer sense of the meaning of Christianity and a larger view of Christ's purpose for mankind. To miss this is to miss the whole splendour and glory of Christ's religion. Next to losing the sense of a personal Christ, the worst evil that can befall a Christian is to have no sense of anything else. To grow up in complacent belief that God has no business in this great groaning world of human beings except to attend to a few saved souls is the negation of all religion. The first great epoch in a Christian's life, after the awe and wonder of its dawn, is when there breaks into his mind some sense that Christ has a purpose for mankind, a purpose beyond him and his needs, beyond the churches and their creeds, beyond Heaven and its saints—a purpose which embraces every man and woman born, every kindred and nation formed, which regards not their spiritual good alone but their welfare in every part, their progress, their health, their work, their wages, their happiness in this present world.

What, then, does Christ do all day? By what further conception shall we augment the selfish view of why Christ lived and died?

Social Side of Christianity

I shall mislead no one, I hope, if I say—for I wish to put the social side of Christianity in its strongest light—that Christ did not come into the world to give men religion. He never mentioned the word religion. Religion was in the world before Christ came, and it lives to-day in a million souls who have never heard His name. What God does all day is not to sit waiting in churches for people to come and worship Him. It is true that God is in churches and in all kinds of churches, and is found by many in churches more immediately than anywhere else. It is also true that while Christ did not give men religion He gave a new direction to the religious aspiration bursting forth then and now and always from the whole world's heart. But it was His purpose to enlist these aspirations on behalf of some definite practical good. The religious people of those days did nothing with their religion except attend to its observances. Even the priest, after he had been to the temple, thought his work was done; when he met the wounded man he passed by on the other side. Christ reversed all this—tried to reverse it, for He is only now beginning to succeed. The tendency of the religions of all time has been to care more for religion than for humanity; Christ cared more for humanity than for religion—rather His care for humanity was the chief expression of His religion....

What Christ came here for was to make a better world. The world in which we live is an unfinished world. It is not wise, it is not happy, it is not pure, it is not good—it is not even sanitary. Humanity is little more than raw material. Almost everything has yet to be done to it.

Before the days of Geology people thought the earth was finished. It is by no means finished. The work of Creation is going on. Before the spectroscope, men thought the universe was finished. We know now it is just beginning. And this teeming universe of men in which we live has almost all its finer colour and beauty yet to take. Christ came to complete it. The fires of its passions were not yet cool; their heat had to be transformed into finer energies. The ideals for its future were all to shape, the forces to realize them were not yet born. The poison of its sins had met no antidote, the gloom of its doubt no light, the weight of its sorrow no rest. These the Saviour of the world, the Light of men, would do and be. This, roughly, was His scheme.

The Program of the Society

HUNDREDS of years before Christ's Society was formed, its Programme had been issued to the world. I cannot think of any scene in history more dramatic than when Jesus entered the church in Nazareth and read it to the people. Not that when He appropriated to Himself that venerable fragment from Isaiah He was uttering a manifesto or announcing His formal Programme. Christ never did things formally. We think of the words, as He probably thought of them, not in their old-world historical significance, nor as a full expression of His future aims, but as a summary of great moral facts now and always to be realized in the world since he appeared.

Remember as you read the words to what grim reality they refer. Recall what Christ's problem really was, what His Society was founded for. This Programme deals with a real world. Think of it as you read—not of the surface-world, but of the world as it is, as it sins and weeps, and curses and suffers and sends up its long cry to God. Limit it if you like to the world around your door, but think of it—of the city and the hospital and the dungeon and the graveyard, of the sweating-shop and the pawn-shop and the drink-shop; think of the cold, the cruelty, the fever, the famine, the ugliness, the loneliness, the pain. And then try to keep down the lump in your throat as you take up His Programme....

A Physician of Humanity

If Christianity could even deal with the world's Depression, could cure mere dull spirits, it would be the Physician of Humanity. But it can. It has the secret, a hundred secrets, for the lifting of the world's gloom. It cannot immediately remove the physiological causes of dulness—though obedience to its principles can do an infinity to prevent them, and its inspirations can do even more to lift the mind above them. But where the causes are moral or mental or social the remedy is in every Christian's hand. Think of any one at this moment whom the Spirit of Heaviness haunts. You think of a certain old woman. But you know for a fact that you can cure her. You did so, perfectly, only a week ago. A mere visit, and a little present, or the visit without any present, set her up for seven long days, and seven long nights. The machinery of the Kingdom is very simple and very silent, and the most silent parts do most, and we all believe so little in the medicines of Christ that we do not know what ripples of healing are set in motion when we simply smile on one another. Christianity wants nothing so much in the world as sunny people, and the old are hungrier for love than for bread, and the Oil of Joy is very cheap, and if you can help the poor on with a Garment of Praise, it will be better for them than blankets.

Or perhaps you know someone else who is dull—not an old woman this time, but a very rich and important man. But you also know perfectly what makes him dull. It is either his riches or his importance. Christianity can cure either of these though you may not be the person to apply the cure—at a single hearing. Or here is a third case, one of your own servants. It is a case of *monotony*.

Prescribe more variety, leisure, recreation—anything to relieve the wearing strain. A fourth case—your most honoured guest: Condition—leisure, health, accomplishments, means; Disease—Spiritual Obesity; Treatment—talent to be put out to usury. And so on down the whole range of life's dejection and *ennui.*

Perhaps you tell me this is not Christianity at all; that everybody could do that. The curious thing is that everybody does not. Good-will to men came into the world with Christ, and wherever that is found, in Christian or heathen land, there Christ is, and there His Spirit works. And if you say that the chief end of Christianity is not the world's happiness, I agree; it was never meant to be; but the strange fact is that, without making it its chief end, it wholly and infallibly, and quite universally, leads to it. Hence the note of Joy, though not the highest on Christ's Programme, is a loud and ringing note, and none who serve in His Society can be long without its music. Time was when a Christian used to apologize for being happy. But the day has always been when he ought to apologize for being miserable.

Christianity, you will observe, really works. And it succeeds not only because it is divine, but because it is so very human—because it is common-sense.

Begin in Your City

IF any one wishes to know what he can do to help on the work of God in the world let him make a City, or a street, or a house of a City. Men complain of the indefiniteness of religion. There are thousands ready in their humble measure to offer some personal service for the good of men, but they do not know where to begin. Let me tell you where to begin—where Christ told His disciples to begin, at the nearest City. I promise you that before one week's work is over you will never again be haunted by the problem of the indefiniteness of Christianity. You will see so much to do, so many actual things to be set right, so many merely material conditions to alter, so much striving with employers of labour, and City councils, and trade agitators, and Boards, and

Vestries, and Committees; so much pure unrelieved uninspiring hard work, that you will begin to wonder whether in all this naked realism you are on holy ground at all. Do not be afraid of missing Heaven in seeking a better earth. The distinction between secular and sacred is a confusion and not a contrast; and it is only because the secular is so intensely sacred that so many eyes are blind before it. The really secular thing in life is the spirit which despises under that name what is but part of the everywhere present work and will of God. Be sure that, down to the last and pettiest detail, all that concerns a better world is the direct concern of Christ.

I make this, then, in all seriousness as a definite practical proposal. You wish, you say, to be a religious man. Well, be one. There is your City; begin. But what are you to believe? Believe in your City. What else? In Jesus Christ. What about Him? That He wants to make your City better; that that is what He would be doing if He lived there. What else? Believe in yourself—that you, even you, can do some of the work which He would like done, and that unless you do it, it will remain undone. How are you to begin? As Christ did. First He looked at the City; then He wept over it; then He died for it.

Where are you to begin? Begin where you are. Make that one corner, room, house, office as like Heaven as you can. Begin? Begin with the paper on the walls, make that beautiful; with the air, keep it fresh; with the very drains, make them sweet; with the furniture, see that it be honest. Abolish whatsoever worketh abomination—in food, in drink, in luxury, in books, in art; whatsoever maketh a lie—in conversation, in social intercourse, in correspondence, in domestic life. This done, you have arranged for a Heaven, but you have not got it. Heaven lies within, in kindness, in humbleness, in unselfishness, in faith, in love, in service. To get these in, get Christ in. Teach all in the house about Christ—what He did, and what He said, and how He lived, and how He died, and how He dwells in them, and how He makes all one. Teach it not as a doctrine, but as a discovery, as your own discovery. Live your own discovery.

Then pass out into the City. Do all to it that you have done at home. Beautify it, ventilate it, drain it. Let nothing enter it that can defile the streets, the stage, the newspaper offices, the booksellers' counters; nothing that maketh a lie in its warehouses, its manufactures, its shops, its art galleries, its advertisements. Educate it, amuse it, church it. Christianize capital; dignify labour. Join Councils and Committees. Provide for the poor, the sick, and the widow. So will you serve the City.

You Are the Key

If you ask me which of all these things is the most important, I reply that among them there is only one thing of superlative importance and that *is yourself.* By far the greatest thing a man can do for his City is to be a good man. Simply to live there as a good man, as a Christian man of action and practical citizen, is the first and highest contribution any one can make to its salvation. Let a City be a Sodom or a Gomorrah, and if there be but ten righteous men in it, it will be saved.

It is here that the older, the more individual, conception of Christianity, did such mighty work for the world—it produced good men. It is goodness that tells, goodness first and goodness last. Good men even with small views are immeasurably more important to the world than small men with great views. But given good men, such men as were produced even by the self-centred theology of an older generation, and add that wider outlook and social ideal which are coming to be the characteristics of the religion of this age, and Christianity has an equipment for the reconstruction of the world, before which nothing can stand. Such good men will not merely content themselves with being good men. They will be forces—according to their measure, public forces. They will take the city in hand, some a house, some a street, and some the whole. Of set purpose they will serve. Not ostentatiously, but silently, in ways varied as human nature, and many as life's opportunities, they will minister to its good....

It is idle to talk of Christ as a social reformer if by that is meant that His first concern was to improve the organization of society, or provide the world with better laws. These were among His objects, but His first was to provide the world with better men. The one need of every cause and every community still is for better men. If every workshop held a Workman like Him who worked in the carpenter's shop at Nazareth, the labour problem and all other workman's problems would soon be solved. If every street had a home or two like Mary's home in Bethany, the domestic life of the city would be transformed in three generations. External reforms—education, civilization, public schemes, and public charities—have each their part to play. Any experiment that can benefit by one hairbreadth any single human life is a thousand times worth trying. There is no effort in any single one of these directions but must, as Christianity advances, be pressed by Christian men to ever further and fuller issues. But those whose hands have tried the ways, and the slow work of leavening men one by one with the spirit of Jesus Christ....

Your Life Is Your Religion

There is an almost awful freedom about Christ's religion. "I do not call you servants." He said, "for the servant knoweth not what his lord doeth. I have called you friends." As Christ's friends, His followers are supposed to know what He wants done, and for the same reason they will try to do it—this is the whole working basis of Christianity. Surely next to its love for the chief of sinners the most touching thing about the religion of Christ is its amazing trust in the least of saints. Here is the mightiest enterprise ever launched upon this earth, mightier even than its creation, for it is its re-creation, and the carrying of it out is left, so to speak, to haphazard—to individual loyalty, to free enthusiasms, to uncoerced activities, to an uncompelled response to the pressures of God's Spirit. Christ sets His followers no tasks. He appoints no hours. He allots no sphere. He Himself simply went about and did good. He did not stop life to do some special thing which should be called religious. His life was His religion. Each day as it came brought round in the ordinary course its natural ministry. Each village along the highway had someone waiting to be helped. His pulpit was the hillside, His congregation a woman at a well. The poor, wherever He met them, were His clients; the sick, as often as He found them, His opportunity. His work was everywhere; His workshop was the world. One's associations of Christ are all of the wayside. We never think of Him in connection with a Church. We cannot picture Him in the garb of a priest or belonging to any of the classes who specialize religion. His service was of a universal human order. He was the Son of Man, the Citizen.

This, remember, was the highest life ever lived, this informal citizen-life. So simple a thing it was, so natural, so human, that those who saw it first did not know it was religion, and Christ did not pass among them as a very religious man. Nay, it is certain, and it is an infinitely significant thought, that the religious people of His time not only refused to accept this type of religion as any kind of religion at all, but repudiated and denounced Him as its bitter enemy. Inability to discern what true religion is, is not confined to the Pharisees. Multitudes still who profess to belong to the religion of Christ, scarcely know it when they see it. The truth is, men will hold to almost anything in the name of Christianity, believe anything, do anything—except its common and obvious tasks. Great is the mystery of what has passed in this world for religion.[3]

REFLECTIONS AND RECIPES
1. Create your own recipe: Christ's Program for Me." List the places you touch regularly that need Christ. Then beside each list any ingredients (talents, experience, training) that can make a difference in those places as you live your life as a good workman.
2. Have you ever thought about what Christ would do if He woke up in your home every day, traveled to your place of business, saw your co-workers, did your assigned work, associated with your friends, and

participated in your family relationships? Take stock of what He might do that is different than what you are doing. (Remember, He isn't announcing that He is God.) If there is room for improvement on your part, place that part of your life before God and ask Him to speak to your heart. Pray for the Holy Spirit to strengthen you to follow-through with His directions.

3. Make a plan to be sensitive to Christ's program for you. To do this you must place every hour as a gift of worship that can glorify Him. Raise your sensitivity throughout your day for divine encounters and divine opportunities. Jesus never saw any circumstances as chance events. They all required a response from the Father, and Jesus did what He saw the Father doing. Go and do likewise.

4. Where has your life turned into mere religious activity? Take each area before the Lord and repent for replacing Him with earthly aspirations that appear good. Don't rush the confession but when release and forgiveness come, embrace them so that you may press on to the next level.

5. "Jesus knew that Martha needed to see past the humanity she served so faithfully to fully perceive and receive His divinity" (*Chasing God, Serving Man*, 36). This provides a paradigm as to how we must judge our own good works. Though many things we do may produce the praise of men, we need to sort out what receives the praise of God. How do you think you can judge between the two? Do you have any good works that need to be released? Are there some good works that you have avoided that God is now calling forth in you?

George MacDonald

George MacDonald (1824-1905) was a Scottish preacher, poet, novelist, fantasist, expositor, and public figure who was most well known for his children's books....

His fame is based on far more than his fantasies. His lifetime output of more than fifty popular books placed him in the same literary realm as Charles Dickens, William Thackery, and Thomas Carlyle. He numbered among his friends and acquaintances Lewis Carroll, Mark Twain, Lady Byron, and John Ruskin.

Among his later admirers were G.K. Chesterton, W. H. Auden, and C.S. Lewis. MacDonald's fantasy Phantastes was a turning point in Lewis' conversion; Lewis acknowledged MacDonald as his spiritual master, and declared that he had never written a book without quoting from MacDonald.

Although in MacDonald's time he was one of Britain's top-selling and most respected authors, in the twentieth century his books eventually became harder and harder to find until the only Mac-Donald books in print were a few of his books for children. After decades of being overlooked, MacDonald is once again a literary and spiritual influence in the lives of thousands of people.[4]

"THE PLACE OF DIVINE SERVICE"

When I use the phrase *divine service*, I mean nothing whatever about the church or its observances. I mean simply serving God. Shall I make the church a temple of idolatrous worship by supposing that it exists for the sake of supplying some need that God has, or of gratifying some taste in him, that I there listen to his Word, say prayers to him and sing his praises for his benefit? Shall I degrade the sanctity of the closet, hallowed in the words of Jesus, by shutting myself behind its door in the vain fancy of doing something there that God requires of me as a sacred observance?

Do not talk of public worship as divine service. Search the prophets and you will find observances, fasts and sacrifices and solemn feasts of the temple were regarded by God's holy men with loathing and scorn just because by the people they were regarded as *divine service*.

I do, however, believe that true and genuine service may be given to the living God. And for the development of the divine nature in man, it is necessary that he should do something for God. And it is not hard to discover how, for God is in every creature and in their needs. Therefore, Jesus says that whatever is done to one of his little ones is done to him. And if the soul of a believer be the temple of the Spirit, then is not the place of that man's labor—his shop, his bank, his laboratory, his school, his factory—the temple of Jesus Christ, where the spirit of the man is at work? The counter ought to be his altar, and everything laid on it with intent of doing as one can for his neighbor, in the name of Christ Jesus.

Never wait for fitter time or place to talk to him. To wait till you go to church, or to your closet, is to make *him* wait. He will listen as you walk in the lane or the crowded street, in a field or in a place of meeting.

Remember that the service he requires is not done in any church. He will say to no one, "You never went to church; depart from me, I do not know you." But he will say, "Inasmuch as you never helped one of my Father's children, you have done nothing for me."

Church is *not* the place for divine service. It is a place of prayer, a place of praise, a place to feed upon good things, a place to learn of God, as is every place. It is a place to look in the eyes of your neighbor and love God along with him, as is every place. But the world in which you move, the place of your living and loving and labor, not the church you go to on your holiday, is the place of divine service. Serve your neighbor, and you serve God.[5]

REFLECTIONS AND RECIPES

1. Create your own recipe: "Divine Service." What are your current acts of divine service? List them. Check off the ones on your list that are performed within the walls of your church. Star the ones on your list that are accomplished outside the walls of your church. Highlight the ones which reflect MacDonald's definition of divine service. Are you pleased or displeased with the results? Why?

2. If public worship is not divine service, what is it? What is its function? Why is it done? Who receives the benefits and why? Is it necessary? Why or why not? Describe the place of public worship in your own life.

3. Give an example in your life when you responded to someone in an act of service and you knew it was a divine "set up" in which the Lord received your service as you did it for that person. How did you know God directly received from your service? How regularly does this type of thing happen to you? In your opinion, how often should you have this experience?

4. If the world is the place of our divine service, then we must have a plan. What should be your strategy for your divine service? Without a plan, you may find nothing changes. With a plan, you will see direction and goals as part and parcel of the process. Create a strategy for your service including measurable goals along the way.

5. "Without Martha's practical Christian service and work ethic operating in your personality, you will find it hard to maintain a godly witness among other people. For some reason, people expect Christians to act selflessly to help others. Many in the Church would rather gather at the river of God for fellowship and gospel singing than gather under the bridge of homelessness to dispense equal servings of food, clothing, and unconditional love to society's 'unlovable untouchables'" (*Chasing God, Serving Man*, 68). In your opinion, why do Christians desire to stand at the river rather than to touch the unlovely? What mind-set needs to be broken? What fears need to be addressed? What reward awaits those who serve the unlovely? Why isn't this reward valued to the point of action?

Dietrich Bonhoeffer

Dietrich Bonhoeffer was born on February 4, 1906, in Breslau, Germany. Later a student in Tubingen, Berlin, and at Union Theological Seminary in New York, Bonhoeffer became known as one of the few figures of the 1930s with a comprehensive grasp of both German- and English-language theology. His works resonate with a prescience, subtlety, and maturity that continually belies the youth of their author.

Bonhoeffer assumed the leadership of the Confessing Church's seminary at Zingst by the Baltic Sea. Out of the experiences at this school emerged his two well-known books, *The Cost of Discipleship* and *Life Together*, as well as his lesser known writings on pastoral ministry, such as *Spiritual Care.*

Bonhoeffer's theologically rooted opposition to National Socialism first made him a leader in the stand agaisnt Hitler and an advocate on behalf of the Jews.

He was hanged in the concentration camp at Flossenbürg on April 9, 1945.

Bonhoeffer proves that to think and to worship are not segregated. In fact, the thinking man worships...even if it costs him his life.[6]

"VISIBLE CHURCH IN A SECULAR WORLD"

This is how the Church invades the life of the world and conquers territory for Christ. For whatever is "in Christ" has ceased to be subject to the world of sin and the law. No law of the world can interfere with this fellowship. The realm of Christian love is subject to Christ, not to the world. The Church can never tolerate any limits set to the love and service of the brethren. For where the brother is, there is the Body of Christ, and there is his Church. And there we must also be....

But "let each man abide in that calling wherein he was called. Wast thou called a bondservant? care not for it: but if thou canst become free, use it rather" (i.e. remain a slave). "For he that is called in the Lord, being a bondservant, is the Lord's freedman: likewise he that was called, being free, is Christ's bondservant. Ye were bought with a price; become not the servants of men. Brethren, let each man, wherein he was called, therein abide with God" (I Cor. 7:20-24). How different it all sounds from the calling of the first disciples! *They* had to leave everything and follow Jesus. *Now* we are told: "Let each man abide in the calling wherein he was called." How are we to reconcile the contradiction? Only by recognizing the underlying motive both of the call of Jesus and of the exhortation of the apostle. In both cases it is the same—to bring their hearers into the fellowship of the Body of Christ. The only way the first disciples could enter that fellowship was by going with Jesus. But now through Word and Sacrament the Body of Christ is no longer confined to a single place. The risen and exalted Lord had returned to the earth to be nearer that ever before. The Body of Christ has penetrated into the heart of the world in the form of the Church....

Let the slave therefore remain a slave. Let the Christian remain in subjection to the powers which exercise dominion over him. Let him not contract out of the world (I Cor. 5:11). But let the slave of course live as a freeman of Jesus Christ. Let him live under authority as a doer of good, let him live in the world as a member of the Body of Christ, the New Humanity. Let him do it without reserve, for his life in the world must be of such a quality as to bear witness to the world's lost condition and to the new creation which has taken place in the Church. Let the Christian suffer only for being a member of the Body of Christ.

Remain in the World

Let the Christian remain in the world, not because of the good gifts of creation, nor because of his responsibility for the course of the world, but for the sake of the Body of the incarnate Christ and for the sake of the Church. Let him remain in the world to engage in frontal assault on it, and let him live the life of his secular calling in order to show himself as a stranger in this world all the more. But that is only possible if we are visible members of the Church. The antithesis between the world and the Church must be borne out in the world. That was the purpose of the incarnation. This is why Christ died among his enemies. That is the reason and the only reason why the slave must remain a slave and the Christian remain subject to the powers that be.

This is exactly the conclusion Luther reached with regard to the Christian's secular calling during those critical years when he was turning his back on the cloister. It was not so much the lofty standards of monasticism that he repudiated, as their interpretation in terms of individual achievement. It was not otherworldliness as such that he attacked, but the perversion of otherworldliness into a subtle kind of "spiritual" worldliness. To Luther's mind that was a most insidious perversion of the gospel. The otherworldliness of the Christian life ought, Luther concluded, to be manifested in the very midst of the world, in the Christian community and in its daily life. Hence the Christian's task is to live out that life in terms of his secular calling. That is the way to die unto the world. The value of the secular calling for the Christian is that it provides an opportunity of living the Christian life with the support of God's grace, and of engaging more vigorously in the assault on the world and everything that it stands for.[7]

ME

REFLECTIONS AND RECIPES

1. Create your own recipe: "Submission Stew." You determine the amounts of each ingredient.

    ____ Obeying speed limits
    ____ Honoring my boss
    ____ Showing respect to officers of the law and politicians in government
    ____ Not wishing for a different set of gifts or talents
    ____ Giving double honor to elders in the church
    ____ Being a great neighbor
    ____ Speech is consistent behind or in front of person who is discussed
    ____ Exhibiting patience with those who are slower or less talented than you
    ____ Not coveting another's position or job
    ____ Consistent display of appreciation of spouse or significant family members

    What ingredients need to be increased in your life? A recipe is only as good as it is used to bring a tasty finale to the process. Allow God to measure the ingredients in your life and add through the power of the Holy Spirit. Though the fires in the oven of your daily walk may be hot, they are necessary to make the final product.

2. How can you be a bondservant and yet be free? Is this an attitude, a reality or wishful thinking? Where in your life do you feel like you are a bondservant to something or someone? (Check those things that produce stress in your life.) How can you sense the freedom you have in Christ in the midst of the "slavery"?

3. The apostle Paul tells us in the First Corinthian passage to remain as you are. Why does God call some to full time ministry and others to other labor? How are they "the same" in God's eyes? How are they different? In what way are both acts of worship?

4. Our Christianity is not complete without the element of its witness. How does your job afford you the opportunity for others to see Jesus in you? How have you seen opportunities come to increase the kingdom of God? How does the visible church conquer the world?

5. "The shortage of field hands is so critical that Jesus commanded us to pray to the Lord of the harvest for more reapers to work in the field of souls. The problem here is that no one wants to "go outside" of the comfortable kitchen in the house of God to work in the fields...(God) knows that He will never lack for field hands if we place our lives in His hands" (*Chasing God, Serving Man*, 92). How many non-Christians do you touch in a day? How many of those do you see almost every day of the week? What impact have you had in their lives? Have you

prepared yourself in the presence of God so that you can effectively reap the harvest set before you?

ENDNOTES

1. www.ccel.org/d/drummond/greatest/htm Reprinted as is.

2. Tommy Tenney, *God Chasers Daily Meditation and Personal Journal* (Shippensburg, PA: Destiny Image, 1999), pp. 86-87.

3. www.ccel.org/d/drummond/greatest/htm/

4. www.johannesen.com/GMD.htm. Used by permission. Reprinted as is.

5. George MacDonald, *Unspoken Sermons, Third Series* (Eureka, CA; Sunrise Books, 1996), "Forgiveness," pp. 227-228. Used by permission.

6. Tommy Tenney, *God's Favorite House Journal* (Shippensburg, PA: Fresh Bread, 2000), p. 57. Also see www.dbonhoeffer.org

7. Dietrich Bonhoeffer, *The Cost of Discipleship* (New York: MacMillan, 1963), pp. 289-290, 296-298. Used by permission.

Chapter Four

Classic Historical Portraits of Compassionate Action

We will now explore the spiritual components that comprise an effective recipe for "touching" the world of humanity. As we look back in time through the window of church history we see a glorious parade of God chasers living in the secret place, empowered by His passionate love, to reach out to those who live on the outer fringes of society. Acts of mercy and manifestations of love characterize these mighty saints of God. The pages of this book could not contain even a small portion of their service of man. So I will attempt to give you only a broad stroke of the brush, painting for you a treasured picture of these awesome servants of man.

A Compassionate Saint and a Loving Mystic

St. Francis—An Instrument of Peace

One of the first followers of the Lord to rediscover the Lord's passion for the poor was St. Francis of Assisi. He was born in 1182, the son of one of the most well-to-do families in Assisi. Occasional incidents in his younger days revealed some intolerance in his heart, but it was on one of those occasions that the seed of his future transformation was planted. One day while working intently in his father's cloth shop arranging the fabric, a beggar came to the door and asked for alms in God's name. Francis rudely kicked the man out, but at once he regretted his actions and followed the man to offer his apologies. This event replayed in his mind over and over again.

Later on in his life, during a brief stay in Rome, he took out his money, took off his garments, and gave them all to the poor. On another occasion he encountered a leper in Assisi and, instead of fleeing as most villagers did, he went up to him and embraced him. He did all this despite the scorn of his friends and his father's great disappointment. His steps before him were ordered; that leper represented Christ Himself! So Francis renounced his father's possessions and went on to work among the poor and leprous people of his time.

Here are the oft-quoted words of St. Francis:

> Lord, make me an instrument of Thy peace;
> Where there is hatred, let me sow charity;
> Where there is injury, pardon;
> Where there is error, the truth;
> Where there is doubt, the faith;
> Where there is despair, hope;
> Where there is darkness, light; and
> Where there is sadness, joy.
> O, Divine Master,
> Grant that I may not so much seek to be consoled, as to console;
> To be understood as to understand;
> To be loved as to love;
> For it is in giving that we receive;
> It is in pardoning that we are pardoned.

MADAME GUYON—A GOD CHASER AND LOVER OF MAN

...Madame Guyon was one of the most outstanding spiritual writers of the 1600s. She was known for her deep spiritual perception and for her pursuit of union with God. Besides her spiritual writings, she also was known for her compassion for the poor and deprived. Read her own words from her autobiography:

"In acts of charity I was assiduous. So great was my tenderness for the poor, that I wished to supply all their wants. I could not see their necessity, without reproaching myself for the plenty I enjoyed. I deprived myself of all I could to help them. The best at my table was distributed among them. Being refused by others, they all came to me.

"God used me to reclaim several from their disorderly lives. I went to visit the sick, to comfort them, to make their beds. I made ointments, dressed their wounds, buried their dead. I furnished tradesmen and mechanics wherewith to keep their shops. My heart was much opened toward my fellow-creatures in distress."[1]

The Free Church Reaches Out to the World

Donald Durnbaugh does an excellent job in presenting the power of the Anabaptists' compassion for their world. That compassion is set in great contrast to the Reformation churches. His book *The Believer's Church* presents one of the best presentations of the impact of the "Free Churches" upon the culture during the times of the Reformation. Their efforts are in many ways the foundations for the church's involvement in the needs of the world. They were some of the first to discover the balance between passionate pursuit of God and compassionate service of man. These quotes from his book will be a source of great motivation and inspiration for you as you read them.

The author of the most comprehensive study of the missionary activity of the Anabaptists has likened them to primitive Christianity in which the bearers of the gospel were largely the common members. "The Reformation churches have scarcely anything like it to set over against the Anabaptist phenomenon." To him the 'astonishing thing about Anabaptism is not so much the activity of ordained leaders…as the missionary commitment of the ordinary members."[2]

…Franklin H. Littell has documented the thesis that the Anabaptists were the first to make the Great Commission the responsibility of every member. There is indeed impressive evidence that most members felt the call to convince and convert others, relatives, neighbors, strangers....

The view of the Reformers was that no preaching could be done unless it was performed by a pastor duly ordained by the state. They called Anabaptists "hedge preachers"....Among the errors listed of the Anabaptists was that "anyone who has a true faith may preach, even if no one has commissioned him: for Christ has empowered any and every man to preach when He said 'Go, teach all nations.'"[3]...

Early Anabaptism had a vision of responsibility for all the world. "They believed that the Church of the Restitution, the True Church with its disciplined laymen, carried history."[4]...

The Quakers clearly had a world vision at the beginning of their life. "Quakerism was a missionary movement before it was an organized religious society."[5]...

Before this the Pietists in Germany had opened a new era in missions....Two young men, recent students at Halle under August Hermann Francke, came to his attention as desiring employment in missions. Their names were Bartholomew Ziegenbalg and Henry Plütschau. The men reached Tranquebar south of Madras in East India in 1705 and began there a mission which for nearly one hundred years was the only Protestant outpost on the subcontinent....

The Renewed Moravian Church under the leadership of Count Zinzendorf, himself a student at Halle, was responsible for the most extensive missionary activity of the eighteenth century. "Here was a new phenomenon in the expansion of Christianity, an entire community, of families as well as of the unmarried, devoted to the propagation of the faith." Their first outreach was to Greenland and to the West Indies, where they were prepared to become slaves, if need be, in order to minister to the Negroes.[6]...

"In two decades the little church of the [Moravian] Brthren called more missions to life than did the whole of Protestantism in two centuries."[7]

Not only had they established themselves in missionary activity around the world, but the "Free Church" were renowned also for their commitment to the social needs of man. They were not content simply to preach the gospel message; like Martha, they were willing to get their hands dirty in their service of man. Again Mr. Durnbaugh speaks to the heart of these great social pioneers.

When Does the Service Begin?

The Quakers tell the story of a stranger who happened to enter a Friends' meetinghouse, expecting the usual Protestant Sunday worship. After sitting in the general silence for ten minutes, the puzzled visitor whispered to the soberly clad person seated next to him: "Excuse me, but when does the service begin?" The answer came back crisply: "Friend, the service begins right after the meeting is over!" This identification of the whole of life with consistent regard for the welfare of other people has been a hallmark of the Friends and other Believers' Churches.[8]...

The unity of their devotional life with social action has captured the admiration of many. A professor at the University of Hull explained why he became a "convinced" Friend. "What particularly appealed to me...was the direct way in which the insistence on the quiet inward life became inevitably associated with its active outward expression in the world of affairs."[9]...

Knowing firsthand the despicable conditions of prisons in England and America, the Quakers agitated for reform. Elizabeth Fry, a quiet and refined lady, braved the incredible clamor and degradation of the women's section of the Newgate Prison in London in 1813 in repeated visits and succeeded in changing for the better the life of the "idle, savage, drunken, unruly women." Quakers in Pennsylvania first developed the concept that prison life should be designed as remedial rather than punitive....

Also remarkable was their attitude toward the insane. Instead of treating them as animals, as was customary, Quakers said that they were mentally ill. In 1796 William Tukes established "The Retreat" in York, England where patients were treated as guests and physical restraints abolished. Therapy was provided by way of handcrafts.[10]

John Woolman, the great American mystic, is another example of the Quakers' great passion for the disenfranchised of society. He was extremely outspoken in his outrage against slavery.

Woolman would often decline to accept hospitality in a home where slaves were kept or would insist upon reimbursing slaves for work done for him personally....[11]

A Mennonite, Peter C. Plockhoy, issued the first public statement in North America against slavery in connection with regulations for a colony on the Delaware: "No lordships or servile slavery shall burden our company."[12]

Quakers were active before the Civil War in running the "underground railway" of assistance to Negroes escaping to Canada, at considerable risk to themselves.[13]

A Shrimp of a Man Brings an End to the Slave Trade

One of the great lights of social reform in the chronicles of history is the British statesman William Wilberforce. Wilberforce would become the key political leader in the abolition of the slave trade. He was a tiny "shrimp" of a man, but he was gigantic in his courage and tenacious in his struggle against a very popular trade. It was a cause that he believed in and to which he dedicated all of his adult life.

William was strongly influenced in his early life by his aunt and uncle who were very much involved in Methodism. He would later declare to his mother that George Whitefield had put something of a fire in his heart that would remain forever. The Methodist had taught him the importance of getting involved in a cause larger than oneself.

For William the cause would be to forever remove the blight of slavery from the face of British history. The fight would be long and arduous, demanding every ounce of energy his soul possessed. There would be times of failure and deep depression when it seemed that he would never win this war. John Newton, the redeemed ex-slave trader, would be a source of tremendous encouragement for Wilberforce in those times of discouragement.

On the fateful day of February 23, 1807, Wilberforce stepped into the Parliamentary House knowing that this was the day. For more than 40 years William had led the charge against the slave trade. This day would be the climax of a life's work. Sir Andrew Romilly stood up to address the House. Every eye was upon him. In referring to the conquests of Napoleon at that time, he would begin:

> "'And when I compare...those pangs of remorse,' continued Romilly, 'with the feelings of which must accompany my honorable friend [speaking of Wilberforce] from this House to his home, after the vote tonight shall have confirmed the object of his human and unceasing labors; when he retires...to his happy and delightful family, when he lays himself down on his bed, reflecting on the innumerable voices that will be raised in every quarter of the world to bless him, how much more pure and perfect felicity must he enjoy, in the consciousness of having preserved so many millions of his fellow creatures, than—'"

Romilly could not finish the speech because the whole House erupted in an ovation of honor for Wilberforce.

At the end of the day the House passed by a vote of 283 to 6 to abolish the slave trade.

From his deathbed, John Wesley wrote concerning Wilberforce, "I see not how you can go through your glorious enterprise in opposing that execrable villainy, which is the scandal of religion, of England, and of human nature. Unless God has raised you up for this very thing, you will be worn out by the opposition of men and devils. But if God be for you, who can be against you?"[14]

Wesleyan Revival Begins Amongst the Poor

George Whitefield was driven by his passion for the poor in England's culture and was the subject of much discussion in the British press. *The Gentleman's Magazine* reported:

> The Rev. Mr. Whitefield...has been wonderfully laborious and successful, especially among the poor Prisoners in Newgate, and the rude Colliers of Kingswood, preaching every day to large audiences, visiting, and expounding to religious Societies. On Saturday the 18th Instant he preach'd at Hannum Mount to 5 or 6000 Persons, amongst them many Colliers. In the Evening he removed to the Common, where...were crowded...a Multitude....computed at 20,000 People.[15]

Whitefield's efforts did not go unnoticed or uncriticized. One alarmed London gentleman warned:

> The Industry of the inferior People in a Society is the great Source of its Prosperity. But is one Man, like the Rev. Mr. Whitefield should have it in his Power, by his Preaching, to detain 5 or 6 thousand of the Vulgar from their daily Labour, what a Loss, in a little Time, may that bring to the Publick!—For my part, I shall expect to hear of a prodigious Rise in the Price of Coals, about the City of Bristol, if this Gentleman proceeds, as he has begun, with his charitable Lectures to the Colliers of Kingswood.[16]

Whitefield sent for John Wesley, recognizing his preaching power and organizing skill. Up to this point, however, Wesley had preached only in regular church services while in England. Should he accept Whitefield's appeal and help with the open-air meetings in Bristol? Charles thought not. But John submitted the decision to the Fetter Lane Society which cast lots and decided he should go.

Wesley's Journal for Saturday, March 31 reads:

In the evening I reached Bristol, and met Mr. Whitefield there. I could scarce reconcile myself at first to this strange way of preaching in the fields, of which he set me an example on Sunday; having been all my life (until very lately) so tenacious of every point relating to decency and order, that I should have thought the saving of souls almost a sin if it had not been done in a church....[17]

The next day, Monday, Wesley reports:

At four in the afternoon I submitted to be more vile, and proclaimed in the highways the glad tidings of salvation, speaking from a little eminence in a ground adjoining to the city, to about three thousand people. The Scripture on which I spoke was this,..."The Spirit of the Lord is upon Me, because He hath anointed Me to preach the gospel to the poor."[18]

Wesley immediately began to organize societies and bands to reach out to the people.

The Wesleyan Revival had begun. From the beginning it was a movement largely for and among the poor, those whom "gentlemen" and "ladies" looked on simply as part of the machinery of the new industrial system. The Wesleys preached, the crowds responded and Methodism as a mass movement was born.[19]

One of Wesley's favorite sayings was: "Go not to those who want you, but to those who want (i.e. need) you most."[20]

Wesley also had a great passion and desire to help the unemployed. In fact his field preaching was a means of giving hope to the factory worker. At the age of eighty-two he spent whole days walking about to collect money for the poor.

How a Revival Started in the Marketplace

In the earlier part of the last century, America thrived. Businessmen and merchants were extremely prosperous and few people felt it necessary to call on God for anything. Not even to praise

Him for His great generosity. Then, it happened. A crash like few others in American history struck the nation, bringing to their knees the same businessmen and merchants who were until recently, celebrating in the streets. Thousands of businesses were forced to close as banks went under and railroads went bankrupt. Huge numbers of employees were forced to the streets looking for work; over 30,000 idle sets of hands in New York City alone. By the fall of 1857, families became desperate and most faced starvation.

During this time, one man was lucky enough to be appointed as City Missionary in downtown New York. Jeremiah Lanphier was appointed by the North Church of the Dutch Reformed denomination. The church's membership was quickly dwindling as people left the city in search of work and housing elsewhere. Jeremiah was commissioned to visit the neighborhood with a goal to reach people and to have them attend the diminishing church. The North Church felt they made an ideal choice of man to serve in this capacity, and so he was.

Jeremiah's heart was burdened by the needs in his area. Families were impoverished all around him and something needed to change. That's when he had an idea and decided to invite those around him to join him in a weekly prayer meeting, to be held on Wednesdays at noon. He distributed the following handbill as an invitation:

How Often Shall I Pray?

> As often as the language of prayer is in my heart; as often as I see my need of help; as often as I feel the power of temptation; as often as I am made sensible of any spiritual declension or feel the aggression of a worldly spirit.

> In prayer we leave the business of time for that of eternity, and intercourse with men for intercourse with God.

> A day Prayer Meeting is held every Wednesday, from 12 to 1 o'clock, in the Consistory building in the rear of the

North Dutch Church, corner of Fulton and William Streets (entrance from Fulton and Ann Streets).

This meeting is intended to give merchants, mechanics, clerks, strangers, and business men generally an opportunity to stop and call upon God amid the perplexities incident for those who may find it inconvenient to remain more than five or ten minutes, as well as for those who can spare the whole hour.

On the 23rd of September 1857, the very first noonday Prayer Meeting was begun! The doors were opened and there stood Jeremiah, alone, and waiting. After a bit of time, Jeremiah began to pace the floor. Was no one in the city coming to pray? At approximately 12:30 he heard footfall on the stair and there the first person appeared, then another and yet another. Soon six people were in attendance at the first Noonday Prayer Meeting. The next week, forty people gathered to pray for their city.

The next month it was decided that a daily meeting would be held. Within six months, over ten thousand businessmen were coming daily to pray in New York, and in two years, over a million followers were added to churches in America.

The prayer of one man, on a Wednesday afternoon in 1857, literally led a spiritual awakening! Do you think you're prayers could do the same thing today? Yes! They can! The God of 1857 is still the God of today, and your prayers are heard just as Jeremiah's were.

The story continues...

In similar situations around the country, revival brought about changes that were astounding:

One owner of a hardware store reported that one of his manufacturers followed him to a noonday prayer meeting and afterward, confessed that he had been cheating the storeowner for years, and wanted to pay back all he had taken.

Notorious criminal "Awful Gardiner" turned his life around through the prayer meetings.

Crime drastically declined in the nation as thousands became followers of Christ and the wealthy helped the poor.

Ships docking at the New York harbor had many passengers converted to Christianity even before debarking.

Shop owners who closed their doors for an hour at noontime, brought customers with them to the prayer meetings, many being converted before leaving to go back to doing business with the merchants.

As men sat in the noontime prayer meetings they began to hear prayer requests for family members to come to know the Lord. One gentleman heard a request from a wife for her husband to be saved and he realized that request came from his own wife! And, he gave his life to the Lord. Yet another man heard a request from a mother, asking for prayers from her unsaved son. The request was from his very own mother! This man, too, gave his life to Christ that day. God was surely moving mightily in the prayer meetings of this revival![21]

The Modern Missionary Movement

The primitive church was born in a burst of evangelistic fervor and missionary activity. Scattered by persecution and famine, the early church went forth preaching the gospel of Jesus Christ into all the Roman empire. As the first century came to a close, the passion for preaching began to dwindle as the church turned inward.

In the 16th century this passion for reaching the world was resurrected in a fury of evangelistic outreach. Let me tell you about a few whose passion for missions has significantly impacted thousands of young people in recent generations.

I'll start with David Brainerd, who exhibits the very heart of this book. He was so committed to prayer that he often hid himself in a cut out log, agonizing in intercession. His passionate prayers transformed him into a compassionate man who gave himself in ministry to the American Indians.

David Brainerd (1718-1747)

He died when still a young man. Only 29. But David Brainerd, a young Puritan who ministered to the Indians, was one of America's most influential missionaries. Though his life was brief, Brainerd's intense, passionate devotion to God affected countless Christians for many generations.

Born in 1718 to a devout Puritan family in Haddam, Connecticut, David Brainerd was orphaned at the age of 14. At twenty-one, swept up by the Great Awakening, he had a conversion experience and enrolled at Yale. Though an excellent student, Brainerd was dismissed in 1742 for criticizing one of the tutors, saying he had no more grace than a chair! Brainerd's regret over his rash statement could not secure his reinstatement. He ever afterward remained sensitive about criticism and maintaining Christian unity.

Brainerd studied with pastor Jedidiah Mills to prepare for the ministry and was soon licensed to preach. He went to work among the Indians at Kaunameek, about half way between Stockbridge, Massachusetts and Albany, New York. He diligently learned the Indian language but had little missionary success. So he moved on.

After being ordained by the Presbytery of New York, he began a new work among the Delaware Indians of Pennsylvania. Here too Brainerd saw little success in his ministry. Though often despondent because of his ineffective ministry, loneliness, and repeated illness brought on by tuberculosis, Brainerd determined to live wholly for God, whatever his outward success.

During 1745-1746, Brainerd traveled to minister to the Indians near Trenton, New Jersey and was amazed at the immediate responsiveness of the Indians to the Christian message. Over 100 Indians at a time came to him in the region. Brainerd poured out his life in ministry to these Indians, writing that he wanted "to burn out in one continual flame for God." He helped secure land for the Indians when theirs was threatened and soon constructed a church, school, carpenter's shop, and infirmary.

By the fall of 1746 Brainerd was increasingly coughing up blood. The famous theologian-pastor, Jonathan Edwards, brought him to his home in Northampton, MA. There David Brainerd spent his last months, succumbing to tuberculosis on October 9, 1747.

Jonathan Edward's daughter Jerusha nursed Brainerd during his last illness, and a deep love developed between them. Edwards once overheard Brainerd tell Jerusha, "If I thought I should not see you, and be happy with you in another world, I could not bear to part with you. But we shall spend a happy eternity together." Jerusha contracted tuberculosis and died a few months after David, at the age of eighteen.

After Brainerd's death, Jonathan Edwards edited and published his diary, describing it as an example of a devotional life "most worthy of imitation." This diary was to influence many missionaries in future generations, including William Carey and Henry Martyn, who went to India and Jim Eliot, the twentieth century missionary who gave his life ministering to the Auca Indians.[22]

William Carey (1761-1834)[23]

"Sit down, young man; when it pleaseth the Lord to convert the heathen, he will do it without your help or mine." The speaker was Dr. John Ryland, respected leader of the British Baptists. One should not be too hard on Dr. Ryland, for his words simply reflected the prevalent thinking of his contemporaries. The young man he was addressing was William Carey, a simple cobbler, teacher and preacher.

Carey's zeal could not to be squelched. In 1792 he published *An Enquiry into the Obligation of Christians to Use Means for the Conversion of the Heathens*. William Carey refused to be shut down by any obstacle. The barriers were many and menacing, any one of which would have given him cause to give up. He endured the hindrances of no formal education, rejection by his peers, family tragedies, slow results and cultural barriers.

Carey chose to respond to the pounding passion in his heart and set off for India where he would establish a mission enterprise near Calcutta. There he formed a team of colleagues whose accomplishments elevated them to a high stature in missions history. Like David Brainerd, William Carey's life would inspire tens of thousands to give themselves for the spread of the gospel.

Hudson Taylor (1832-1905)

Hudson Taylor was born in Yorkshire, England in 1832. After a brief period of teenage skepticism, he came to Christ by reading a Christian tract in his father's apothecary store. A few months after his conversion, he consecrated himself wholly to the Lord's work. He sensed the Lord was calling him to China, and he began studying medicine and lived on as little as possible, trusting God for his every provision.

In 1853, the twenty-one-year-old Taylor sailed for China as an agent of a new mission society. He arrived in Shanghai the next spring and immediately began learning Chinese. Funds from home rarely arrived, but Taylor was determined to rely upon God for his every need, and he never appealed for money to his friends in England. Repeatedly he later told others, "Depend upon it. God's work, done in God's way, will never lack for supplies."

In those days, foreigners were not allowed into China's interior; they only were allowed in five Chinese ports. Hudson Taylor, however, was burdened for those Chinese millions who had never heard of Christ. Ignoring the political restrictions, he traveled along the inland canals preaching the gospel....

By 1860, foreigners were able to legally travel anywhere in China, missionaries were allowed, and the Chinese were permitted to convert to Christianity.

At a time when tremendous opportunities were opening up in China, ill health forced Taylor, with his wife and small daughter, to return to England. What seemed at first to be a setback in his mission work turned out to be a step forward. While in England recovering his health, Taylor was able to complete his medical studies. He revised a Chinese New Testament and organized the China Inland Mission. The Mission's goal: To bring the gospel where it had never been brought before.

Twenty-two people accompanied Taylor back to China in 1866. They were aware of the "utter weakness in ourselves, we should be overwhelmed at the immensity of the work before us, were it not that our very insufficiency gives us a special claim to the fulfillment of His promise, 'My grace is sufficient for thee; My strength is made perfect in weakness.'"

The sufferings and hardships multiplied: Taylor's daughter died from water on the brain; the family was almost killed in the Yang Chow Riot of 1868; Maria, Taylor's first wife, died in childbirth; his second wife died of cancer; sickness and ill health were frequent. Yet, the China Inland Mission continued its work of reaching China's millions for Christ. By 1895 the Mission had 641 missionaries plus 462 Chinese helpers at 260 stations. Under Hudson Taylor's leadership, C.I.M. had supplied over half of the Protestant missionary force in China. During the Boxer Rebellion of 1900, 56 of these missionaries were martyred, and hundreds of Chinese Christians were killed. The missionary work did not slack, however, and the number of missionaries quadrupled in the coming decades.

Chinese Christians proved remarkably resiliant under Communism. They did not die out but multiplied many-fold in one of the greatest expansions in church history.[24]

C.T. Studd (1860-1931)

Over a hundred years ago, in February 1885, a group of young men set sail from England to become missionaries in China. They included graduates and ex-army officers and were known as the "Cambridge Seven" because they had felt called to the mission field after attending meetings at that University. The leading member of the group was Charles T. Studd, the son of a wealthy indigo-planter who had retired from India to a large country house at Tidworth in Wiltshire....

Charles and two of his brothers, Kynaston and George, were all at Eton when their father was converted and they were far from pleased by his efforts to interest them in the gospel. However, unknown to each other, all three were also converted when a visiting preacher went to stay with the Studd family during the summer holidays of 1878. The three brothers excelled at cricket both at Eton and later at Cambridge where they achieved a remarkable record of each captaining the cricket team in successive seasons from 1882 to 1884....

Charles was increasingly burdened and convicted by verses such as "Ask of me, and I shall give thee the heathen for thine inheritance, and the uttermost parts of the earth for thy possession." (Psalm 2:8). Although his friends and relatives tried to dissuade him, Charles knew he was being called to the mission field and he sought an interview with Hudson Taylor, the director of the China Inland Mission and was accepted as an associate member.

Studd's decision was followed by six others within a few weeks and as they prepared for the mission field, members of the "Cambridge Seven" spoke at meetings up and down the country with remarkable results. In addition to numerous conversions a great wave of missionary zeal swept through the students of Edinburgh, London, Oxford and Cambridge which was to have profound effects throughout the world in later years.

For C. T. Studd those future years were to see him giving away his family inheritance to help the work of George Muller, D.L. Moody, Dr. Barnardo and others and spending ten years in China where he suffered great hardships to reach remote areas where the gospel had never been heard before....

...Studd became concerned about the large parts of Africa that had never been reached with the Gospel and in 1910 he went to the Sudan and was convicted by the lack of Christian witness in central Africa. Out of this concern Studd was led to set up the Heart of Africa Mission and when challenged as to why he was preparing for a life of inevitable hardship he replied, "If Jesus Christ be God and died for me, then no sacrifice can be too great for me to make for Him."

On his first venture into the Belgian Congo in 1913, Studd established four mission stations in an area inhabited by eight different tribes. Then a serious illness to his wife required his return to England, but when he returned to the Congo in 1916 she had recovered sufficiently to undertake the expansion of the mission into the World Evangelism Crusade with workers in south America, central Asia and the middle East as well as Africa. Supported by his wife's work of home, Studd built up an extensive missionary outreach based on his centre at Ibambi and although she made a short visit to the Congo in 1928 that was the only time they met again since she died in the following year. Two years later, still labouring for the Lord at Ibambi at the age of seventy, Charles Studd died, but his vision for China, India and Africa had expanded to reach the whole unevangelised world.[25]

REFLECTIONS AND RECIPES

Read It and Weep

This chapter should thrill your heart with the exploits of "favorite" saints who paved the way for our modern ministry and mission. But it should send you to the tissues as you grasp the callousness of contemporary hearts that rarely receive such bounty from God's will and even less rarely see the world with eager eyes in order to strike change wherever their foot falls. Where are our St. Francises and our Wesleys? Why are you and I not at maximum compassion on our mercy meters? Sacrifice as a way of life seems rather unseemly in this age of self expression. Warning: The exercises below may necessitate change.

1. Create your own recipe: "Giving It All." Follow St. Francis of Assisi's recipe. Personalize it with your own life opportunities....What will you give? Who will you embrace? Etc.

   Mix together

   Give your money to the poor
   Embrace a person with AIDS

Apologize to the ones you've offended
Give clothing and possessions to the needy
Sow charity instead of hatred

2. Madame Guyon was known for her compassion for the poor and deprived. When was the last time you saw or touched a poor person first hand? Plan a trip either to a community mission, a soup kitchen, or a homeless outreach. Search your heart as you serve those in need around you. When is someone "too dirty" for you to touch? When are they "too smelly" to be around? When is someone "too lazy" to make something out of themselves? Find the seat of judgment in your own heart and mind and ask God to place His perspective on that seat. You may need to repent. But more than likely, God will challenge you to the next level of compassion and require you to express love outside your comfort zone.

3. William Carey was a man who refused to be shut down by any obstacle. The barriers and hindrances that would have turned many away from such a goal as he had, did not render a response from Carey. What obstacle do you face in your life in regards to fulfilling a mission or purpose that God desires? Where are barriers or hindrances creating a devotion toward procrastination for you rather than a surrendering to the timely will of God? Take your day planner and place your mission goal on every Monday throughout the next three months. Each Monday, set aside time to address each hindrance or obstacle. Some may be outwardly real, but others may have inward implications alone. Dare to not shut down!

4. "Ask of me and I shall give thee the heathen for thine inheritance…" This was a verse of conviction for C.T. Studd. What "heathen" has God given you for your inheritance? What is your responsibility toward unbelievers? What sacrifice are you willing to make to reach these, even if it costs you some dignity? Begin to name the "heathen" God has specifically given to you in your prayer time each day. Transcend the "quick mention" technique to where you pour out to the Father on their behalf and grow to love them as Jesus does.

5. "Compassion played a crucial role in the miracles Jesus performed during His ministry. It seems to me that many of the greatest miracles occurred serendipitously; they just seemed to 'happen' in the course of everyday events. Jesus would see a problem and basically say, 'I have to do something about it' " (*Chasing God, Serving Man*, 60). Pray for Christ's compassion to blossom in your life in a new way. Ask for His creativity to enter in so that you will see others with His compassion and know how to respond in mercy and grace. Become a living miracle as God's divine encounters come to life with those who live their lives around yours.

ENDNOTES

1. Donald L. Milam, Jr., *The Lost Passions of Jesus.* (Shippensburg, PA: Mercy Place, 1999), pp. 127-128. Used by permission.

2. Donald Durnbaugh, *The Believers' Church.* (New York: The MacMillan Company, 1968), p. 232, quoting Wolfgang Schäfele, "The Missionary Vision and Activity of the Anabaptist Laity," *Mennonite Quarterly Review*, XXXVI (1962), pp. 99-115. Used by permission of Herald Press, Scottdale, PA. Reprinted as is.

3. Durnbaugh, p. 233.

4 Durnbaugh, p. 234, quoting Franklin H. Littell, *Anabaptist View of the Church.* , p. 109.

5. Durnbaugh, p. 234, quoting D. Elton Trueblood, *The People Called Quakers.* (New York: Harper and Row, 1966), p. 247.

6. Durnbaugh, p. 235.

7. Durnbaugh, p.236, quoting Warneck, p. 63

8. Durnbaugh, p. 265.

9. Durnbaugh, p. 273, quoting Trueblood, p. 256.

10. Durnbaugh, pp. 273-274.

11. Durnbaugh, p. 274.

12. Durnbaugh, pp. 274-275, quoting Leland Harder, "Plockhoy and Slavery in America," *Mennonite Life*, VII (October 1952), 187-189.

13. Durnbaugh, p. 275.

14. Donald L. Milam, Jr., *The Lost Passions of Jesus*, pp. 129-130. Used by permission.

15. Howard A. Snyder, *The Radical Wesley and Patterns for Church Renewal.* (Downers Grove IL: Inter-Varsity Press, 1980), p. 32, quoting *The Gentleman's Magazine*, 9 (May 1739), p. 257. Used by permission.

16. Snyder, p. 32, quoting "Of the Pernicious Nature and Tendency of Methodism," *The Gentleman's Magazine*, 9 (May 1739), p. 257.

17. Snyder, p. 33, quoting *The Journal of the Rev. John Wesley, A. M.*, ed. Nehemiah Curnock (London: Epworth, 1909-16; rpt. 1938), II, p. 167.

18. Snyder, p. 33, quoting Wesley, *Journal*, II, pp. 172-173.

19. Snyder, p. 33.

20. Rupert Davies, *Methodism.* (New York: Penguin Books, 1963), p. 67.

21. "America's Greatest Spiritual Awakening; How Revival Started in the Marketplace," 03 Dec 2001, www.lighthousesatwork.org/lamphier.htm Used by permission. Reprinted as is.

22. www.gospelcom.net/chi/GLIMPSEF/Glimpses/glmps)79.shtml Used by permission. Reprinted as is.

23. The section on William Carey adapted from "William Carey's Amazing Mission," Glimpses, no. 45, (Worcester, PA: Christian History Institute), 12 Dec 2001, © Christian History Institute, www.gospelcom.net/chi/GLIMPSEF/glimpses/glmps045.shtml

24. "Hudson Taylor: A Heart for China's Millions," *Glimpses*, no. 47, (Worcester, PA: Christian History Institute), 03 Dec 2001, © Christian History

Institute www.gospelcom.net/chi/GLIMPSEF/glimpses/glmps047.shtml Used by permission. Reprinted as is.

25. "All for Christ," *The Christian Bookshop: C.T. Studd* 1862-1931, Copyright © 1997, Heath Christian Book Shop Charitable Trust, 03 Dec 2001, www.christian-bookshop.co.uk/free/biogs/ctstudd.htm Used by permission. Reprinted as is.

Chapter Five

Contemporary Devotional Thoughts for Compassionate Action

Now we turn our eyes from the window of church history to look into our own living rooms, searching for contemporary ingredients to add to our recipe of compassion.

How wonderful it is to start with President George W. Bush. He has led the charge rallying the armies of compassion. His words and actions have been a great source of inspiration for many of us.

We will also blend in the writings of my good friend Bart Pierce, Dr. Marva Mitchell, and Rich Marshall. These are not just preachers of compassion. They are involved in compassionate ministry. Let their words be mixed into the fiber of your soul.

Rallying the Armies of Compassion

President George W. Bush

America is rich materially, but there remains too much poverty and despair amidst abundance. Government can rally a military, but it cannot put hope in our hearts or a sense of purpose in our lives.

Government has a solemn responsibility to help meet the needs of poor Americans and distressed neighborhoods, but it does not have a monopoly on compassion. America is richly blessed by the diversity and vigor of neighborhood healers: civic, social, charitable, and religious groups. These quiet heroes lift people's lives in ways that are beyond government's know-how, usually on shoestring budgets, and they heal our nation's ills one heart and one act of kindness at a time.

The indispensable and transforming work of faith-based and other charitable service groups must be encouraged. Government cannot be replaced by charities, but it can and should welcome them as partners. We must heed the growing consensus across America that successful government social programs work in fruitful partnership with community-serving and faith-based organizations—whether run by Methodists, Muslims, Mormons, or good people of no faith at all.

The paramount goal must be compassionate results, not compassionate intentions. Federal policy should reject the failed formula of towering, distant bureaucracies that too often prize process over performance. We must be outcome-based, insisting on success and steering resources to the effective and to the inspired. Also, we must always value the bedrock principles of pluralism, nondiscrimination, evenhandedness and neutrality. Private and charitable groups, including religious ones, should have the fullest opportunity permitted by law to compete on a level playing field, so long as they achieve valid public purposes, like curbing crime, conquering addiction, strengthening families, and overcoming poverty....

The Problem

Our Nation has a long and honorable commitment to assisting individuals, families, and communities who have not fully shared in America's growing prosperity. Yet despite a multitude of programs and renewed commitments by the Federal and state governments to battle social distress, too many of our neighbors still suffer poverty and despair amidst our abundance.

Consider:

•   As many as 15 million young people are at risk of not reaching productive adulthood—falling prey to crime, drugs and other problems that make it difficult to obtain an education, successfully enter the workforce, or otherwise contribute to society;

- About 1.5 million children have a father or mother in prison;

- Over half a million children are in foster care, more than one fifth of whom are awaiting adoption;

- In 1997, more than one million babies were born to unwed mothers, many of them barely past their own teen years; and

- More than one out of six American families with children live on an annual income of $17,000 or less.

Millions of Americans are enslaved to drugs or alcohol. Hundreds of thousands of our precious citizens live on the streets. And despite the many successes of welfare reform, too many families remain dependent on welfare and many of those who have left the rolls can barely make ends meet.

A great and prosperous nation can and must do better. Americans are a deeply compassionate people and will not tolerate indifference toward the poor. But they also want compassionate results, not just compassionate intentions.

Welfare Reform

The American people support a vital role for government, but they also want to see their Federal dollars making a real difference in the lives of the disadvantaged. Americans believe our society must find ways to provide healing and renewal. And they believe that government should help the needy achieve independence and personal responsibility, through its programs and those of other community and faith-based groups.

To achieve these goals, Federal assistance must become more effective and more tailored to local needs. We must not only devolve Federal support to state and local governments where appropriate, but move support out to neighborhood-based caregivers.

Traditional social programs are often too bureaucratic, inflexible, and impersonal to meet the acute and complex needs of the poor. Reforms must make the Federal Government a partner with faith-based and community organizations that are close to the needs of people and trusted by those who hurt. These organizations boast uncommon successes, but they are outmanned and outflanked.

Building on Success

This Administration proposes a different role for government in social policy—a fresh start and a bold new approach. We will realign Federal policy and programs to better use, empower, and collaborate with grassroots and nonprofit groups. We will reinforce and support programs that work and increase their scale.

We must continue to ask: What are the Federal Government's social responsibilities? What budget should be allocated to social programs? These are vital questions. Yet equally vital is the question of how the Federal Government should fulfill its social task. In social policy, the independent sector—secular and religiously affiliated providers, civic groups, foundations and other grant-givers—has long been an indispensable and valued partner of government. We seek to add to, not take away from, their good work.

We will focus on expanding the role in social services of faith-based and other community-serving groups that have traditionally been distant from government. We do so not because of favoritism or because they are the only important organizations, but because they frequently have been neglected or excluded in Federal policy. Our aim is equal opportunity for such groups, a level playing field, a fair chance for them to participate when their programs are successful. We will encourage Federal agencies to become more hospitable to grassroots and small-scale programs, both secular and faith-based, because they have unique strengths that government can't duplicate.

The Federal Government must continue to play a prominent role in addressing poverty and social distress. But that role must move beyond funding traditional, non-governmental organizations. Americans deserve a rich mix of options because when it comes to conquering addiction, poverty, recidivism, and other social ills, one size does not fit all....

Faith-Based and Community Organizations

Starting now, the Federal Government is adopting a new attitude to honor and not restrict faith-based and community initiatives, to accept rather than dismiss such programs, and to empower rather than ignore them.

In welfare and social policy, the Federal Government will play a new role as supporter, enabler, catalyst and collaborator with faith-based and community organizations. We will build on past innovations, most notably bipartisan Charitable Choice legislation, but move forward to make Federal programs more friendly to faith-based and community solutions.

This initiative is not anti-government, but pro-results. It is designed to make sure that faith-based community-serving groups have a seat at the table. It will eliminate the federal government's discrimination against faith-based organizations while also applauding and aiding secular nonprofit initiatives. It will reach out to grassroots groups without marginalizing established organizations. America has a strong, thriving nonprofit sector. Recent figures indicate that the 1.4 million organizations comprising the independent sector receive over $621 billion in total annual revenue, representing six percent of the national economy. Charities and other nonprofits employ over 10 million individuals, comprising over seven percent of the American workforce.

Our goal is to energize civil society and rebuild social capital, particularly by uplifting small non-profit organizations, congregations and other faith-based institutions that are lonely outposts of energy, service, and vision in poor and declining neighbor-hoods and rural enclaves.

Without diminishing the important work of government agencies and the wide range of nonprofit service providers, this initiative will support the unique capacity of local faith-based and other community programs to serve people in need, not just by provid-ing services but also by transforming lives.[1]

REFLECTIONS AND RECIPES

1. Create your own recipe. Have a piece of paper beside you throughout the day. Jot down what you do with simple cues so you will remember.
   Example:
   Drove to work
   Got coffee
   Responded to my email
   Met with my supervisor
   Several exchanges with my subordinates
   Gave project information to team for composite
   Etc.

At your evening time with God, take this list before Him and thank Him for what He did to make your day successful. Praise Him for His nature and character that became evident as you needed His wisdom to solve problems or His strength to be diligent. Lift your hands in wor-ship and let Him declare what He sees in your list. He may speak about how tomorrow needs to be different. He may reward you with His blessing on something you did. He may declare a secret as to how you obeyed His voice and so thwarted the enemy.

2. Using your talents to the glory of God not only affords you the blessing of seeing God at work through you, but it prevents others who do not have those talents from being placed in a position where you need to be. Extol God for the talents and gifts He has given you. Take time to dedicate each one anew to His use. Give them back to the Lord so He can use them as He chooses.

3. Where does your ministry stop? What is its boundary? Is it the walls of your church or "classical religious activity"? How do you need to allow the Holy Spirit to infiltrate your job, your relationships, and your hob-bies with His purpose? Pray that tomorrow will carry more of His mark on each thing you do.

4. Assimilating the character of Christ into all areas of life and society is more than a matter of the will. It is performance of what has been stored

up within the heart. How much does your devotional time spill over to your daily life? What part of your life is easily affected by it? What seems hard to connect to your time with God? Do you find your godliness dissipates as time takes you further away from the morning walk with God? In what ways is God asking you to change?

5.   "Martha leans harder on the strength and provision of God when she finds herself in the place of prayer, praise, worship, and spiritual service. Her discomfort and insufficiency drives her closer to the Rock of her life"(*Chasing God, Serving Man*, 87). As long as Martha's source for her strength and faithful service comes from her Savior, she will be renewed and refreshed as she serves. When she replaces the Lord with busy-ness and good works, she will tire quickly and burn out. What does your emotional energy meter read in regards to your job? Your ministry? Your family relationships? If your energy seems low, you are not putting the right fuel in your tank. Ask God to show you how to take the hard things you do and put them under His easy yoke.

Seeking Our Brothers

BART PIERCE

from *Seeking Our Brothers*[2]

I am convinced that reaching out to society's "throw-aways," the outcasts, and the destitute, the "ones nobody wants," is fundamental to the gospel. It is certainly a defining characteristic of genuine followers of Christ. Jesus Himself made this clear in the parable of the sheep and the goats.

> *And He will set the sheep on His right hand, but the goats on the left. Then the King will say to those on His right hand, "Come, you blessed of My Father, inherit the kingdom prepared for you from the foundation of the world: for I was hungry and you gave Me food; I was thirsty and you gave Me drink; I was a stranger and you took Me in; I was naked and you clothed Me; I was sick and you visited Me; I was in prison and you came to Me." Then the righteous will answer Him, saying, "Lord, when did we see You hungry and feed You, or thirsty and give You drink? When did we see You a stranger and take You in, or naked and clothe You? Or when did we see You sick, or in prison, and come to You?" And the*

King will answer and say to them, "Assuredly, I say to you, inasmuch as you did it to one of the least of these My brethren, you did it to Me" (Matthew 25:33-40).

In the eyes of Jesus, ministering to the poor, needy, and destitute in His name is the same as ministering to Him. On the other hand, rejecting or ignoring the needy is the same as rejecting or ignoring Jesus (see Mt. 25:41-45). For those supposed followers who refused to show compassion, Jesus had only words of judgment: "Then He will also say to those on the left hand, 'Depart from Me, you cursed, into the everlasting fire prepared for the devil and his angels'...And these will go away into everlasting punishment, but the righteous into eternal life" (Mt. 25:41,46).

Make no mistake about it: this kind of ministry is tough and it can be messy. You can't reach out to someone like Curtis without getting your hands dirty. Sometimes it means providing a bath or helping someone find a job. Sometimes, as with Curtis, it even means a set of false teeth. Compassion ministry means doing whatever is necessary to meet the need, and that requires getting outside the four walls of the church building. We can't take care of the hurting and hungry in the carpeted convenience of our comfort zones. We cannot afford to wait for them to come to us; we must go to them.

Somehow much of the modern Church has gotten things turned around. Far too often we avoid or turn our backs on the needy and destitute because it is hard work and there is very little "glory" in it, at least by man's standards. It *is* not what the typical "ministry" today likes to do. Besides, ministering to the needy can be expensive. It can "drain" a church's "limited" resources on people who most likely will give little in return. For churches with such a mind-set this would be "pouring good money after bad." Yet we simply cannot ignore the example of Jesus Himself. If we are serious about calling ourselves disciples of Christ, then we must "put our money where our mouth is" with regard to reaching the needy.

By all accounts, Jesus spent much more time among the broken and hurting than He did in the synagogue, the local house of worship.

In fact, on at least one occasion in His own hometown of Nazareth, Jesus was *thrown out of* the house of worship! Ironically, He had just finished publicly defining His mission in terms of ministering to the needy. Reading from the scroll of Isaiah, Jesus said,

> *The Spirit of the Lord is upon Me, because He has anointed Me to preach the gospel to the poor; He has sent Me to heal the brokenhearted, to proclaim liberty to the captives and recovery of sight to the blind, to set at liberty those who are oppressed; to proclaim the acceptable year of the Lord* (Luke 4:18-19).

He then proceeded to rebuke the people for their unbelief. Stung by Jesus' words, the others in the synagogue sought in anger to kill Him, but He walked away (see Lk. 4:20-30).

Jesus was neither afraid nor embarrassed to be seen in the company of the poor and the hungry, the sick and the destitute, or to be thought of as "a friend of tax collectors and sinners" (Lk. 7:34b). After all, that is why He came! "Those who are well have no need of a physician, but those who are sick. I did not come to call the righteous, but sinners, to repentance" (Mk. 2:17b). We have a mandate from Jesus, by His own words and example, to take care of society's "throwaways."

A Heart for the City

For over 16 years Rock City Church has been committed to reaching the city of Baltimore with the gospel of Jesus Christ. This is both my personal passion as pastor and the corporate passion of the congregation as a whole. Our vision is to reclaim the city from despair, spiritual blindness, and the stranglehold of the enemy. The name *Baltimore* means "circle of Baal" and is derived from the ancient pagan worship of the Druids in pre-Christian England and Ireland. There is even a section of the city known as Druid Hill Park. We believe that God has planted our church in Baltimore to help release the city from satan's grip and open the way for God to pour out His blessing and reveal His glory.

Many churches and denominations have virtually given up trying to reach the cities of our nation. In effect, they have written off the cities, surrendering them to the gangs and the drugs, to crime, poverty, and hopelessness. I am convinced that God has a heart for the cities of the world because that is where so many people live. In fact, God's desire and intention to reach the cities is at the "heart" of the divine outpouring of grace, blessing, power, and glory that He is releasing in many parts of the world in our time.

By turning its back on the cities, much of the Church is now looking in the wrong places and has forgotten the example of Jesus. Jesus didn't go after the social "elite," the people with money or power or influence. He didn't pursue those who were "beautiful" in the eyes of the world. Instead, He sought out rough, dirty fishermen like Peter and Andrew, James and John, blind beggars like Bartimaeus, hated tax collectors like Matthew and Zacchaeus, and sick people like lepers and the woman who had been hemorrhaging for 12 years. Once He even revealed the nature of true worship, not to the priests at the temple, but to a woman of ill repute who had been married five times and even then was "shacking up" with a man. Jesus was constantly reaching out to the people that "polite" society considered unworthy of attention.

In the 14th chapter of Luke, Jesus tells the story of a man who gave a great banquet but when the time arrived, all the invited guests made excuses as to why they could not come.

> *...Then the master of the house, being angry, said to his servant, "Go out quickly into the streets and lanes of the city, and bring in here the poor and the maimed and the lame and the blind." And the servant said, "Master, it is done as you commanded, and still there is room." Then the master said to the servant, "Go out into the highways and hedges, and compel them to come in, that my house may be filled. For I say to you that none of those men who were invited shall taste my supper" (Luke 14:21-24).*

As Christians we are called to go out "into the streets and lanes of the city" and "into the highways and hedges" to reach the lost, especially those whom society has written off. The tragedy is that too often the Church has written them off as well.

God's heart is to redeem, restore, and bless the cities, and we must learn to have the same heart. Instead, most of us look at our cities and curse them. We complain about traffic and crime and other problems; we condemn our cities; we do everything except bless them. In Jeremiah 29:7 God commanded the Israelites who had been carried into exile to "seek the peace of the city where I have caused you to be carried away captive, and pray to the Lord for it; for in its peace you will have peace." We may not be living in exile today, but our responsibility to pray for our cities remains. How we speak about our city and how faithful we are to pray for our city will have a direct bearing on the quality of life and peace in the city for ourselves and for everyone else. We must cultivate a heart of compassion for our cities, and that compassion must be born out of a personal and collective passion for the Person and presence of the Lord Jesus Christ and for His glory and honor to be revealed.

REFLECTIONS AND RECIPES

1. Create your own recipe: "Remedy for Unbelief."

     The ingredients to this recipe are found in Luke 4:18-19
     _____ is upon Me
     because _____ Me
     to _____ to the _____
     He has _____ Me to _____ the _____
     to _____ to the _____
     and _____ to the _____
     to _____ those who are _____
     to _____ the _____ of the Lord.

    And the secret ingredient God is using in this recipe is a two letter word that describes by way of a personal pronoun the one sent...
    _____!!! Unbelief stands in our way to complete this recipe for world-change. Confess your unbelief right now and begin speaking this Scripture over your life each day. Ask God to make you a "believer."

2. Do you have a "heart for your city?" In your own words, define what characteristics a "heart for your city" would exhibit. Look at your

definition. What is God speaking to you about your intercessory stance in prayer for the city in which you live? What is He declaring of His will that you might do in a practical way for your city? He may confirm what you are presently doing or press you onward to a new place of burden for the people and government surrounding you.

3.   How do you see the church "writing off" the lost in the city? If God's heart is to "redeem, restore, and bless the cities," how must we stop "cursing" them and instead "bless" them? Take this to a personal level. How must you begin to bless your city verbally? How can you lead others to begin blessing it as well? Take a prayer walk in a strategic part of your town, speaking the Word of God in blessing over it. What does God reveal to you during this walk? These thoughts from God will become a directive for you to bless your city in the following days and weeks.

4.   Bart Pierce says, "For those supposed followers who refused to show compassion, Jesus only had words of judgment: 'Then He will say to those on the left hand, Depart from Me, you cursed, into the everlasting fire prepared for the devil and his angels. And those will go away into everlasting punishment, but the righteous into eternal life' (Mt. 25:41,46)...In the eyes of Jesus, ministering to the poor, needy, and destitute in His name is the same as ministering to Him. On the other hand, rejecting or ignoring the needy is the same as rejecting or ignoring Jesus (Mt. 25:41-45)." How have you acted more like a goat than a sheep according to Matthew 25? How will you change?

5.   "Some churches never affect their communities. They've given the people who live in them a distinct impression that says, in effect, 'That church couldn't care less about us. All they care about is God, and he doesn't seem to care about us either or the folks who claim to be His people would show it.' These churches have no credibility with their communities because they have no works to back their words" (*Chasing God, Serving Man*, 134). Assuming you are a member of a local church, rate your church's community effectiveness according to your standards. Do not judge your leadership, but discern how you can make a difference. What need-meeting ministry could use your help to make a more powerful impact? Become a change agent!

It Takes a Church to Raise a Village

DR. MARVA MITCHELL

from *It Takes a Church to Raise a Village*[3]

An old African proverb asserts, "It takes a village to raise a child." In that village the child entered a society of order, experienced the comfort of its security, and learned the power of its established morality. The village provided leadership founded in integrity and exercised with moral character. In that cultural setting, R-E-S-P-E-C-T was more than a pop song—it was an expected way of life. When the village was in order, it was able to raise talented and stable children who reflected the values of the village.

In Hillary Clinton's book, *It Takes a Village*, she clearly characterizes some of the conditions of a village capable of raising children in a positive environment. She accurately insists that no family is an island and states, "...the society is our context; we do not exist in a vacuum."[4] The environment that our children grow up in leaves its marks on their future lives. Therefore, the condition of the village plays a fundamental part in their spiritual and social development.

Unfortunately, over the last few generations we have watched the gradual deterioration of our precious village. With much pain and grief we must all agree that the village in which we live is in deep need of major renovation—physically, socially, economically, and spiritually.

Where are the true role models for these desperate kids? Society's leaders are perceived as only concerned about their own political agendas, and their moral values are suspect. Entertainers and sports figures have emerged as the cultural "pop" heroes of this new generation, but the message they deliver is confused, materialistic, selfish, and often violent. Pornography pours into our homes through the television and the Internet, tearing at the moral fiber of the village wall. These deteriorating conditions have resulted in a further breaking down of the family and a general disrespect for life. Regrettably, the village has abandoned the children, leaving them unsupervised and hopelessly alone....

The village is no longer qualified or adequately prepared to raise a child because the village itself must be raised. How can the village be rescued? Who or what will it take to raise the village? There can only be one answer to this question: *It Takes a Church to Raise a Village!*

If the Church is to raise the village, it must stop *having* church and start *being* the Church. We can no longer have church as usual.

The Church must come out from behind its walls and begin to impact the village through a display of the love of Christ and a demonstration of the power of Christ. Inside our walled fortresses we have carried out our religious exercises—singing our songs, praying our prayers, preaching our sermons, giving our money—while the village lies in ruins all around us.

Church, this is our day! We must rise up and take responsibility for the village. The government alone is unable to save the village. They are now turning to the Church for help, and the Church must take this responsibility. At the same time the Church must turn to her Lord for a new empowerment and a fresh filling of His love. It is the Church who is called to be light to the world. It is the Church who must set the godly example. It is the Church who must establish integrity and biblical standards. The Church possesses the wisdom and power to raise the village and set a new course for the future. Now the Church must rise up and shake off the collected dust of indifference and inadequacy to face the challenges that are before us.

The Bible says, "Where sin abounded, grace did much more abound" (Rom. 5:20b). The power and penalty of sin has raised its hideous head in our village. That head must be cut off cleanly and decisively by a compassionate demonstration of God's grace. Grace is not a theological thought; it is a vibrant reality exhibited in loving acts of mercy and expressed through the empowering presence of the Lord. We must arise as administrators of the grace of God and become practitioners of the Word of God.

There are more opportunities for the Church than ever before. Congress has passed laws, such as "The Personal Responsibility and Work Opportunity Reconciliation Act of 1996," to release churches to interact with the community. This bipartisan act includes a "Charitable Choice" provision, affording the opportunity for government funding to be received by churches and other religious groups, to help lift families out of poverty. We have no excuse to stay in our comfort zones.

A cloud of misery and apathy overshadows the village surrounding the Church. Our youth are referred to as "Generation X" and labeled as predators. They are stuck in a slough of despair and are powerless to move toward their predestined potential. The Church needs to become a distributor of hope in Jesus Christ. We hold the keys to their destiny, and it is time to unlock the prison doors and let the village prisoners free. It is only the Rock of Christ that can provide a solid place upon which to stand when all other ground is sinking sand.

Isaiah 61:1-3 states,

The Spirit of the Lord God is upon me; because the Lord hath anointed me to preach good tidings unto the meek; He hath sent me to bind up the brokenhearted, to proclaim liberty to the captives, and the opening of the prison to them that are bound; to proclaim the acceptable year of the Lord, and the day of vengeance of our God; to comfort all that mourn; to appoint unto them that mourn in Zion, to give unto them beauty for ashes, the oil of joy for mourning, the garment of praise for the spirit of heaviness; that they might be called trees of righteousness, the planting of the Lord, that He might be glorified.

The village is filled with the oppressed and brokenhearted. A spirit of heaviness pervades the cultural atmosphere. Too many sit at the frightful edges of our religious reach untouched by the love of our living Lord. Now is the time to stand up and extend our hands to these victims, lifting them up into the loving arms of the Lord who can heal them and give them a living hope. Are we prepared to bind up the brokenhearted, loose the captives, cover the naked, and drive off the spirit of heaviness with shouts of glorious praise? We are filled with the Spirit of God and now must release our compassion and anointing on these disenfranchised ones. Let's position ourselves to raising the standard of life in the village rather than maintaining our religious status quo. We have a mandate to touch the world beginning with our own village. We cannot expect others, such as financial corporations, social agencies, or government institutions, to do it. *It takes a Church to Raise a Village!*

The Church has been given the greatest opportunity since the writing of the Book of Acts to significantly alter the state of the village. Our tools for renovation are the love of Christ, the truth of the gospel, and the power of the Spirit. A divine summons has been issued from Heaven. Angelic forces have arrived at the door of the Church urging us to respond quickly. We are being compelled by the Spirit of God to give a dream to the destitute, to provide new desires for the downtrodden, and to deliver a stimulus to the skeptical and a purpose to the pariah of society.

What a glorious day for the Church! We must seize this moment. This is our day to raise the village. It's time to become a spring in the desert and stop preaching to the choir. It's time to die to ourselves that others might be raised up in newness of life.

Let's put aside our doctrinal differences and selfish schemes and agree that Jesus is the answer. The village is dying while we are debating. We spend too much time tearing each other apart when we should be putting the village back together. Our strength is our unity, and it is the great passion of the Lord that we be one. We are all the Body of Christ and together we are forged into a formidable force that cannot be resisted. We must begin to walk out our faith and believe that we can make a difference in turning the village around....

Are we ready to say, "Enough is enough"? Are we ready to come out of hiding and become ambassadors for the gospel? Let us move forward in the confident understanding that:

It Takes a Church to Raise a Village!

REFLECTIONS AND RECIPES

1. Create your own recipe: "A True Role Model for Kids." What ingredients are necessary in a person who is a model for what children should become?

    Mix together
    1.
    2.
    3.
    4.
    5.

What ingredients are not necessary, but if added can "flavor" a person so that a child will want to become like them? In regards to the mix above, how do you see yourself? Do you have the necessary qualities? Do you have the "flavoring" that attracts children to you? Pray over these thoughts right now to give the Lord opportunity to speak to your heart as to how you can increase these ingredients.

2. Dr. Marva Mitchell proposes that entertainers and sports figures, who have emerged as heroes of this generation, deliver confused, materialistic, selfish, and often violent messages. Go to a place that sells teen magazines. Buy one and look at the people who are interviewed, the ads that are displayed, and the topics discussed. Become an informed intercessor and begin to pray over the culture of our teenagers.

3. Do you feel a responsibility to "raise" the village within the four walls of your church? Ask your children's director for a list of the children in the church and begin to speak their names before Father God. When you see a child misbehaving without a parent around, do you intervene and become a "village parent"? Do you greet the children in your church or are they merely attachments to the skirts of their mothers? Begin to make eye contact with them. Get down on their level literally and speak blessing to them.

4. How out of touch are you with the children that enter your space? Make a date with two children to go for lunch. Find out what they like. Find out what the discrepancy is between your "pretension" about these children and the "reality" that truly exists. Do you have expectations and requirements that are unrealistic theory? How must the Holy Spirit change your mind-set to give you a place in the lives of the children you have selected?

5. "God takes you to Martha's kitchen when He has work to be done in the *earthly realm* with willing hands and a compassionate heart. He moves you into Mary's position when He needs something done in the *heavenly realm* with a passionate heart and hands raised in praise and adoration" (*Chasing God, Serving Man*, 85). Make these statements applicable to your own life in regards to the next generation. What is God asking you to do on earth for His children? What is God speaking to you in regards to the heavenly realm in order to change the next generation? You are the village!

God @ Work

RICH MARSHALL

from *God @ Work*[5]

Do business till I come (Luke 19:13b)....

We need to start dreaming bigger dreams, and making bigger plans. Ed Silvoso has affected my thinking on this matter. His book *That None Should Perish*, is about reaching cities through prayer evangelism. During my early years as a pastor, my major goal was for our church to grow. There is certainly nothing wrong with that, but if it stops there, we will miss God's greater desire. God wants us to reach our city, not fill our church building.

Even though we eventually filled our building on Sunday morning, and grew to two, three, and finally four services each Sunday, we were not reaching our city; and anything short of city transformation is unsatisfactory. Many of my pastor friends have discovered that as well and now also focus on reaching their cities.

You can imagine my joy when I found a Bible passage with this exact focus, and which gives the authority for reaching the city to business leaders. The city was Jericho, but it could just as easily be your city. The city-reacher in this case was Jesus. Let us visit the city of Jericho and watch Jesus in action. He has a powerful word for business leaders.

Chapter divisions in the Bible are sometimes not helpful, and I think this is the case in Luke chapter 19. Let us begin reading at Luke 18:35 so we don't miss some valuable insights into Jesus' method for reaching the city.

Jesus came to Jericho accompanied by a crowd. As He was entering the city, a blind man sat by the roadside, begging. Luke does not tell us his name, but from Mark's account we know his name was Bartimaeus. As he heard the multitude coming his way, he asked what was going on. Being informed that Jesus was coming his way, he began to cry out to the Lord. However, those who followed Jesus on that day (could they be likened to the Church?) warned him to be quiet.

I have been a pastor for long enough to know that schedules and programs are "really important." But I have missed God many times because I would not be deterred from time constraints or established programs. It would appear that the crowd around Jesus was acting a lot like I have.

To them it was more important to stay on schedule than to accommodate a poor, begging, blind man. They must have thought they were assisting Jesus in keeping to His agenda, and were committed to getting Him to Jericho on time. But usually it is not His agenda that we are interested in; it is our own agenda.

Jesus was not in a hurry, not at all. The truth is that this man was a part of His agenda, His target audience in the city of Jericho. Jesus' first priority upon entering the city was the poor. A beggar received His full attention, and no other issue could take precedence. Jesus stopped everything to see what He could do for the blind beggar.

God Meets Our Greatest Needs

It strikes me as interesting that the man was begging, and yet when asked by Jesus what he wanted, he made no reference to money or food. He knew enough about Jesus to request the higher need: "Lord that I may receive my sight" (Lk. 18:41b). If Jesus were to look you in the face, and ask you, "What do you want Me to do for you?" what would you say? You need to think about it, because it is in the Father's heart to give you your desires. Have you learned to ask Jesus for the higher thing, or are you still simply asking Him for money and food. Listen to your prayers and see what it is that you are asking the Lord for.

It is a little disconcerting to realize that more fasting is done for money and resources than for souls. Bartimaeus knew that he had a higher need and went for that, his sight. In the process, he received not only his sight but his other needs as well, as we will see in a few moments.

Once Jesus had healed the man, the crowd accepted him, and were willing to welcome him into their midst. Earlier, they were not so excited about bringing in a man with an obvious need. "Oh Lord, help us see the hurting through Your eyes, to focus on the poor as a first priority in our target audience."

As we walk with Jesus along the road to Jericho, we see His next priority. Coming into the city, He was confronted by a rich man named

Zacchaeus (see Lk. 19:1-10). He had the same problem that blind Bartimaeus had—he could not see. In his case, it was not blindness that caused his lack of sight, but instead it was the crowd. They were so tightly packed around the Savior that those on the outside could not see Him.

Many times we believers are so happy inside the four walls of the church, that even those in our own neighborhoods have trouble seeing Jesus in us. How can they? We are never out in the streets. Ministry has become more a process of hiding behind the walls of our buildings than in making Jesus visible in our neighborhoods. Like those surrounding Jesus, we can be more of a detriment than a help in assisting Jesus in the fulfillment of His plan for the city.

Now notice this: Jesus did not target only the poor; He was equally interested in the rich. "Lord, help us to see that the rich are also hurting, and need to see Jesus."

Both groups are equally important to Him, and I believe that it is the Lord's desire for the poor and rich to worship together, to stand next to each other as they lift their praise to the Lord, learning to serve Him together. As I have studied the roles of the kings in the Old Testament, I've found one of the major callings was to lift injustice and to remove oppression. The kings are to be leading out in ministering to the poor.

As Zacchaeus came down from his perch in the tree—the only place he could find to get a glimpse of Jesus—the disciples encountered another problem. Jesus invited Himself to dinner with this sinner. I guarantee you that if you stick around most congregations long enough, you too will forget what it is to associate with sinners.

Making Sinner Friends

Most of my friends are pastors, missionaries, and church leaders. I need some sinner friends! (I said that in one church in Monterrey, Mexico, and was surprised when a girl raised her hand. I asked her what she wanted and she said, "I will be your sinner friend." After the service I talked to her and found that she was a non-Christian, and a first-time visitor to the church. In the same way I needed a sinner friend, she needed a Christian friend.) That is why I am so thrilled that God is raising up a new group of leaders for this coming move of God. Those of you who serve the Lord in the marketplace are already accustomed to daily contact with unbelievers. It makes sense, does it not, that the Lord would choose to use those in the closest contact with the harvest to bring that harvest in?

Jesus was not afraid to make friends of sinners, whether they were poor or rich. They were the ones that He first sought out in Jericho. I have to believe He does the same today, in my city and yours. It is time for us to begin to focus on the same audience. The ones who do not yet know the Lord need to experience His love. And Jesus was able to do this without any condemnation. You will not see Him explaining to either Bartimaeus or Zacchaeus that they are lost and going to hell. Instead, we see Jesus ministering love and compassion. To the blind man, He asked, "What do you want Me to do for you?" (Mk. 10:51) To Zacchaeus He simply said, "Today salvation has come to this house, because he also is a Son of Abraham" (Lk. 19:9).

Reaching Out to Your Own—Miracles Can Happen!

Zacchaeus made some very significant decisions about his lifestyle very early in his relationship with Jesus. We do not know what Jesus said to him, if anything, but simply being in the presence of Jesus caused this man to do some very radical things.

While the disciples were still fuming over the fact that Jesus was associating with a sinner, the sinner in question was doing some very spiritual things. He immediately decided to give half his goods to the poor. The Bible does not tell us that Jesus told him to do that. He might have, but it is also possible that He mentioned nothing at all. I have certainly experienced times when simply being in the presence of Jesus caused me to do some significant things. Whatever the process, whatever means the Lord used to impact Zacchaeus, the result was that he was giving to the poor.

Imagine the reaction of the crowd which included, of course, those that had followed Him into the city of Jericho, and the recently healed blind man who had been sitting by the roadside. When Zacchaeus started looking for the poor to give money to, he would not have had to look far. It is not farfetched at all to presume that Bartimaeus would have been one who received that day.

Think of the moment when Jesus asked the poor man what He could do for him. If the man had simply asked for money, he conceivably could still be sitting by the road, blind and lost, but with a few dollars in his pocket. However, he was healed, walking with Jesus, and receiving his financial needs as well. Remember, Jesus is well able to take care of all your needs, but He may not do it by the process that you have prescribed, or even by a way that seems most likely to you. If He can minister healing to the blind beggar and then minister another kind of healing to a man who will start giving him money, don't you think He can take care of your needs as well?

Zacchaeus was not content with giving away just 50 percent of his money. In addition to that, he also gave back four times whatever he had taken by false accusation. Here was a rich man that had been touched to the very core of his being. For Zacchaeus, becoming a follower of Jesus meant giving away more than half of his money, and he trusted God to meet his needs as he gave....

As far as we know, Zacchaeus did not pray the sinner's prayer. There is no instruction noted in the Bible for the process by which his salvation came to pass. In fact, the only thing we know for sure is that Jesus impacted his heart and his response was to give financially. But the next verse of Scripture tells us that salvation came to his house that day.

Using Your Money for God

It is in that context that we come to a very interesting parable, a parable for the businessperson (see Lk. 19:11-27). Here Jesus' audience included those who followed Him into Jericho, plus those whom He picked up on the way. One of them was a poor blind beggar. One of them was one of the richest men in town, Zacchaeus. Both of them had their lives radically changed by the power of the Lord. Both of them, and I'm sure by this time, everyone else, were ready to hear whatever He had to say. Jesus began talking about money.

Most business leaders understand the concept of making money. Far above any other reason, that is why businesses are started. Hopefully, you have discovered that there are higher purposes for your life, and that you are no longer living with only the desire for money driving you.

It is interesting to note that Jesus had a parable set aside for the businessperson, and that parable was about making money. From this parable, I believe we can learn that Jesus wants us to make money. However, because of the very context of the parable, we know He is concerned about far more than our money. He is looking for people like Bartimaeus and Zacchaeus.

In this parable, we have the story of a certain man who went into a far country. He called ten of his servants together and gave a mina to each one of them. A mina is a sum of money that is equal to about three months' wages. Upon giving the money to his servants, he said to them, "Do *business* till I come" (Lk. 19:13)—instructions for a business and professional person. Any time you receive an amount of money with the command, "Do business till I come," you will obviously realize the serious nature of the situation. It is time to become creative and strategic. You must invest well, work hard, plan right, and do whatever it takes to "do business" with that money.

Taking Authority Over Cities

In this parable, like so many others, some of the workers did well and some did not. But what captures my attention is what the reward was for the man who took the one mina and earned ten minas. We see in verse 17: "Because you were faithful in very little, have authority over ten cities."

Authority over cities! That is what you can gain from faithful business practices—authority in your city, and in nine cities surrounding you. Do you see the tremendous impact of this truth? When God gives you the grace to increase, to make money, He has a purpose for this. His purpose is not only to allow you to gain more, and live easier. His purpose goes beyond even the ability to give more.

He wants to give you authority!

There is tremendous authority in business today. The decision-makers and power brokers in our nation are business leaders who are looked upon as successful. There was a day when the "clergy" were looked to for advice and direction, and in some nations the military or government may carry the authority. But in America today, it is success in the business realm, economic success, that causes people to want to listen to you.

Jesus has put something in your hand: an amount of money perhaps, or an idea, or a strategy for marketing success. As He blesses this, and the one turns into ten, remember that the authority you gain is for the Kingdom. He wants you to impact cities. I originally challenged you to see your marketplace position as your ministry; but Jesus moves it several notches higher. His goal for you is *authority in the city*. Jesus is concerned about your city, your state, and your nation. And He wants to use you to impact your city for the gospel.

The time has come for the kings of the Lord to take their God-given role and change our world. We have waited too long for change to come about through political process. The Republicans take all the credit they can and cast blame on the Democrats. Simultaneously, the Democrats do the same with their particular political agenda. But caring for the poor is not a political issue; it is a Christian issue. God is putting the mandate on the shoulders of the kings to lift the oppression, care for the poor, and bring about justice and mercy in our land. This authority, this God-given authority, must be carefully and prayerfully administrated. God is raising you up for such a time as this.

This parable is not about planting churches. There are no missionary plans, nor can a single priest be found. But God is at work, using business principles and business leaders to impact entire cities for the gospel. Think about it. With just a few ten-mina leaders and another handful of five-mina leaders, we can take dozens, hundreds, even thousands of cities for Christ.

Now let's make a quick review. Jesus came to the city with an eye on the poor and rich. He brought both into the Kingdom, despite the objections of His followers. In the context of that particular crowd, the poor, the rich, the recently healed and blessed, the recently convicted, Jesus told His business parable. Business and professional leaders, don't miss the point. Yes, He wants to bless your business; He wants to help you make money; and He wants to give you authority. But it is also clear from Scripture that He wants to use you to change the status of the poor. When the poor of the inner cities and the CEOs of commerce in those same cities get together, God will release His strategic plan for impacting the cities.

Authority—Not Ability

The plan of God is connected to the authority that He will give to you. Let's think about that for a few moments because it is another key to your success in the kingly anointing. Remember, that anointing comes from the Holy One and abides in you. God takes this anointing and connects it to authority. That is an important point, because authority is something that God gives you based on His sovereignty. When we are called to accomplish something for the Lord, we may complain about our lack of ability; but God is not looking at your ability. He is focusing on the authority that He has given you.

Remember when David was first anointed as king? He was the least likely of all his brothers to be chosen. But then the Word of the Lord came, "Man looks at the outward appearance, but the Lord looks at the heart" (1 Sam. 16:7b). We could paraphrase it this way: "Man looks at ability, but the Lord looks on the heart, knowing the authority that He will place there." You cannot argue with God. Don't try to tell Him that you can or cannot do something based on your ability. I have seen many leaders with great ability fail, because they lacked in anointing; and I have seen people of seeming little ability prosper greatly because of the anointing.

Authority!

Jesus said to His disciples, "Behold, I give you the authority...over all the power of the enemy" (Lk. 10:19a). I would much rather have authority than ability, because the anointing of God connects to that authority and "nothing shall be impossible for you who believe" (see Mk. 9:23). Those who walk in the authority of God will lead this coming marketplace revival. There will always be those who make more money than you do, and there will always be those who have more ability. But when you walk in the authority of God, nothing can stop you....

We need to start responding to God based on His call and on His authority, not based on our ability or our understanding. Oftentimes we have no idea of what God is about to do; however, when we simply walk in obedience, He will bring about the fulfillment of His plan.

Do you see what the Lord has in mind for your business? He wants to bless it so that you gain authority. Then He wants to take the authority and add His anointing to it, so that entire cities are transformed. Although many congregations and mission agencies are involved in city-reaching plans, such as Harvest Evangelism, Mission America, and others, and there is broad cooperation in reaching these major population areas, we still need the involvement of business and professional leaders. Come on, kings! We need you to help usher in the coming city-transforming move of God!

REFLECTIONS AND RECIPES

1.   Create your own recipe: "Do Business 'til I Come." (Luke 19:13b) What does God mean by this? What are the critical ingredients needed to "do business" in the way the Lord expects us to do?

    Mix together
     1.
     2.
     3.
     4.
     5.

Reflect on the ingredients above. How would God see your effectiveness in the business realm? How does Luke 19:13b give you authority to reach those in business? Do you operate in this authority?

2.   How important is your daily schedule? Do you plan well? Are you one who sticks to the schedule "religiously" or do you tend to "go with the flow"? Both have an agenda and produce their own effectiveness. Put your schedule on the altar before the Lord and ask Him to reshape it.

Let Him create the structure or the spontaneity He desires to allow you the most opportunities to hear His Spirit during the day and do what you see the Father doing.

3. Time has become a commodity more valued than money. Everyone is "in a hurry" and most are "stressed out." How much of these issues are self-imposed in your life? Do you have time for God's priorities? Have you spent time asking Him for His priorities for your week or day? God is asking us to STOP EVERYTHING and see what we are to do. As Jesus is our example, take time to go off by yourself and pray. Use a personal day for a private retreat away from the business and home to clear the debris and create a day planner made in Heaven!

4. Rich Marshall writes, "Those of you who serve the Lord in the marketplace are already accustomed to daily contact with unbelievers. It makes sense, does it not, that the Lord would choose to use those in the closest contact with the harvest to bring that harvest in?" What keeps you back from being the laborer in this harvest? Be honest with your own fears, personality issues, skills, etc. Ask the Lord to give you practical ways to overcome these obstacles so that you might be a reaper for God's kingdom.

5. "In every situation, the best thing you can do is ask the Lord, 'What can I do? Where do You want me to be and serve?' Sometimes you need to ask your (opposite) (someone who is not like you in calling or gifting) what you can do" (*Chasing God, Serving Man*, 116). Who is an "opposite" in your life that might give you direction for centering your time, schedule, priorities, and efforts within your work environment? Make an appointment to share and receive from that person.

ENDNOTES

1. George W. Bush, "Rallying the Armies of Compassion," 03 Dec 2001, www.whitehouse.gov/news/reports/faithbased.html

2. Bart Pierce, *Seeking Our Brothers*. (Shippensburg, PA: Fresh Bread, 2000), pp. 3-7. Used by permission.

3. Marva Mitchell, *It Takes a Church to Raise a Village*. (Shippensburg, PA: Treasure House, 2001), pp. xix-xxvi. Used by permission.

4. Marva Mitchell, quoting Hillary Rodham Clinton, *It Takes a Village*. (New York: Simon & Schuster, 1996), 32.

5. Rich Marshall, *God @ Work*. (Shippensburg, PA: Destiny Image, 2000), pp. 43-55. Used by permission.

Chapter Six

CONTEMPORARY PORTRAITS OF COMPASSIONATE CHRISTIANITY

I had the privilege of working closely with my good friend Pastor Bart Pierce in Baltimore for more than three years. Early in our relationship, it became obvious that the grace of God's presence hung heavy over services at Rock City Church. I remember one night puzzling over this in Bart's den. We realized that what was happening in Baltimore was unique because it combined intense, passionate worship with intense, passionate social outreach. He asked the question, "How can we convey that to the people?" As if by revelation it came to me:

Jesus loved both Mary and Martha. These two sisters hosted Jesus in their home, and the Scriptures give us detailed accounts of two of those visits. Mary was a worshiper—most suppose that this is the very same Mary who broke the alabaster box on Jesus' feet and wiped them with her hair. Martha was a servant—she is the one who looked after Jesus' practical and physical needs. In John 11:5 we're told that Jesus loved Martha *and her sister*—in this instance, Jesus Himself gives special attention to Martha.

I may be "Mary" by nature, but that doesn't completely relieve me of "Martha" duties. Bart Pierce may be "Martha" by nature, but as the passion of this book reveals, he also knows what it is like to worship at Jesus' feet. There is a little bit of Martha and a little bit of Mary in both of us.

In this chapter I want to share some of the outrageously compassionate ministry that is being accomplished in cities across our country.

I'll start with some of the exciting things that my friend Bart Pierce is doing in Baltimore and then go on to other equally exciting spiritual feats performed by the spiritual "Marthas" of our generation.

It Takes a Church to Raise a Village

The following two sections, on Nehemiah House and The Hiding Place, are from Bart Pierce, *Seeking Our Brothers* (Shippensburg, PA: Fresh Bread, 2000).

NEHEMIAH HOUSE

Nehemiah House really had its beginning in the late 1980s when we opened a small shelter for men. This was not obedience to some "thus sayeth the Lord" command, but simply a response to an existing need. God *had* charged us to "take care of the ones nobody wants," and as we set out to do so, they came. Homeless men showed up, needing help and a place to stay. Operating such a shelter was almost second nature to me. I had run a halfway house for men in the mid 1970s and, because of my background, I could relate well to them. During my wild dope and surfing days, drug addicts and homeless men had been some of my best friends.

Initially, our youth pastor was in charge of the shelter. The house itself, which belonged to a man in the church, needed a lot of work. It looked as though it had been bombed out. There were areas on the second floor where we couldn't allow an oversized person to walk, for fear that he might fall through. It was a place to start, however, and was good enough for a bunch of guys who desperately needed somewhere to get off the street, be delivered from their drug or alcohol addiction, and get their lives right with God. It wasn't long before God began to open up this ministry in amazing ways.

One day a local Christian businessman asked me to help him with a vision that he had for assisting battered women. At the time, he was working with the county to purchase a piece of property to build transitional housing for these women. At his request I accompanied him to a meeting with a county official to discuss his plan. I went as a favor to him and to provide moral support; I had no official status in the meeting. God had other ideas.

As the two men talked, the county official suddenly stood up and said in frustration, "I'm tired of working with you. You've dragged your feet long enough." I sat there thinking, *Lord, what am I doing here? This is not where I want to be.* The county official went on. "Do you know what I need? I need a shelter for men."

Since I had just opened one, I spoke up. "Well, I just opened one." He looked at me for a moment, then instructed his secretary to make an appointment with me. Turning back to me he asked, "Will you come see me?" I don't know whatever became of the home for battered women, but a couple of days later I was back in his office to discuss a homeless shelter.

His first words to me were, "Reverend, can you do it?" I replied, "Yes, I think so." Then he asked, "Does this really work? Do people's lives really change? Do they really get off drugs?" We talked a little longer and he asked me to return with some specific information. He was not a Christian and was looking for evidence of real people who had kicked drugs or alcohol and who had gotten their lives cleaned up.

Two weeks later I returned to his office, bringing with me a man from our church who was a professional builder. We laid open before him a whole portfolio full of pictures and testimonies of some of the "regular people" in our church who had been released from bondage to drugs, alcohol, prostitution, stealing, and other things. They weren't hard to find. They were serving as my assistant pastors, church leaders, secretaries, janitors—you name it. I did not include my own picture or story, for fear of completely blowing him away!

The county official examined the portfolio, then looked at me. With amazement in his voice he asked as he had two weeks before, "Do you really think you can do this? Does this really work? I've never met anyone who has truly been delivered from this kind of lifestyle of drugs and crime." So, I told him *my* story. As I related my tale of anger, drugs, jail, being shot at, and how Christ had saved me from it all, his eyes got bigger and bigger. Just as I was beginning to wonder if I'd made a huge mistake he said, "How much money do you need to build this shelter?"

The building contractor who was with me gave a figure of $300,000. "That's no problem," the official replied. "Money is not an issue; homelessness is. It's growing every day and we've got to do something about it." By this time I was really getting excited about this meeting! We left his office with a definitive plan to build a shelter for homeless men.

When the time came for us to receive the money, the county official called me. "We may have a problem," he said. I thought, *Oh boy, here's the catch.* "The check was written for $351,000 instead of $300,000. Is that a problem?" I assured him *very* quickly that it was *no* problem at all!

That was in 1991. Since then, we have built three times. The original, old, "bombed out" house is where the men in Phase Three (transitional phase) now live, and today it is as nice a place as you could find. Over the years we have received from Baltimore County, including operational funds, more than 1.7 million dollars for Nehemiah House.

Until this year, the shelter housed 31 men (including four in Phase Three transition), serving over 22,000 meals a year. The recent completion of a new addition has almost doubled our capacity, providing housing for another 25 men. Hundreds of men have been transformed by Christ and established in the Kingdom of God through the ministry of Nehemiah House. Husbands and fathers have been reunited with their wives and children. Other former residents have started successful businesses of their own. Some members of the staff of Nehemiah House, including the current director, are also former residents and participants in the program.

The greatest thing of all, however, is to see many of these men standing in the sanctuary Sunday after Sunday with their hands lifted up and their tears streaming down as they worship their Heavenly Father. Nothing can outdo that! *Does this really work? Absolutely!*[1]

THE HIDING PLACE

The Hiding Place opened in 1986 as a place of refuge for women in crisis situations. Most are young, unmarried, and pregnant. Some are addicted to drugs or alcohol. Many harbor deep hurt and anger, particularly toward men. All are at a place in life where they have nowhere to turn. Abandoned and often abused by their boyfriends (or husbands, fathers, grandfathers, brothers, etc.), or rejected by their families, these young women enter the Hiding Place with little understanding of a stable family environment. Quite often they have no clue either of how to care for the baby they will soon give birth to, or of how to live as godly women. The Hiding Place exists to address all of these needs.

The Hiding Place is a seven-bed residential facility where women in crisis receive love, care, and encouragement in a healthy, Christian family environment, with the emphasis on *Christian* and *family*. It provides a home for many who have never had a real home. Women who enter the program are established in a home structure with a daily routine of work and recreation. All residents take part in the normal domestic chores and activities necessary for keeping house: washing dishes, doing laundry, mopping floors, etc. They learn how to plan and prepare meals, and mealtimes are opportunities for fellowship, questions, discussion, and sharing. The directors of the home, who live at the facility with their family, take part in the everyday life and activity of the home, right along with the residents. It truly is a *family* environment.

Providing a strong Christian atmosphere at the Hiding Place is the highest priority. The only sure and certain answer to the life problems of these women is found in Christ, and they are surrounded with opportunities to know Him and follow Him. Organized Bible study is part of the daily routine of the women. They also have regular opportunities to attend church and participate in church-related activities. Through this environment of Christian love and emphasis on spiritual truth, most of the women who come to the Hiding Place discover during their stay the transforming power of Christ in their lives.

The Hiding Place is not simply a shelter for women in need. It is a fully organized program designed to minister to the physical, emotional, and spiritual needs of the residents. Each woman who enters the program has a wide range of services available to her, including:

• Advocacy—A support person or family is assigned to every woman at the Hiding Place, to befriend, encourage, and assist her during her stay. A pregnant woman in the program is assigned a specially trained helper who will accompany her to the hospital at the time of delivery and remain with her until after the baby is born.

• Homemaking—Each resident receives training in basic domestic skills through participation in household chores and in meal planning and preparation.

• Recreation—Leisure time is important for developing the whole person, so regular "fun" activities are planned, such as family outings, shopping trips, sporting events, handcrafts, and hobbies.

• Medical—Local physicians and nurses volunteer their services to provide medical care for the house residents. Expectant mothers receive both prenatal and postnatal care.

• Education—Each woman is encouraged to continue her education during her stay. Tutoring and guidance in academic matters are provided for this purpose.

• Counseling—Residents of the program receive assistance in discovering how best to develop their individual gifts, talents, and abilities in order to provide for a successful future.

In addition, the program at the Hiding Place includes "Buds to Roses," a nine-month Christ-centered Life Skills curriculum that was developed to help nurture, encourage, and build up women in crisis and give them the natural and spiritual tools they need to reach their full potential in life. Divided into three "trimesters," this program begins with basic and fundamental issues such as self-image and domestic skills, and advances the women to progressively higher levels of confidence, ability, and maturity. At the heart of "Buds to Roses" is the Life Plan, drawn up during the first trimester, in which each woman describes her personal aspirations and dreams and develops a clear and specific plan for attaining her goals. The entire "Buds to Roses" curriculum is designed to help them achieve their goals and realize their dreams.

Since its beginning almost 15 years ago, the Hiding Place has seen over five hundred girls and young women come through its doors. Some were as young as 14 years old. Over 350 babies have been born to the house. It is truly a "refuge in the storm," where women who have been battered by life can find a safe harbor in which to mend their sails, reorient their compass, get their lives together, and chart a new course with Christ as their Pilot.[2]

Reach the Inner Cities of America

DREAM CENTER

It is a well-known fact that one of the first things to be driven from a desperate person is their dreams. Hope is alive as long as a dream is alive. Many in America have little to hope for and dreams are snuffed out. Is it any wonder that the Dream Center awakens in many the dreams they have put in hibernation due to poverty, addiction, homelessness, and most of all, a lack of faith in Jesus Christ?

The Dream Center, founded by Tommy and Matthew Barnett, is the "Martha arms" of Los Angeles International Church. This soul-winning ministry presents the life-changing, uplifting Gospel message through its worship services and through Biblical training, food, clothing, housing, education, and job training to thousands of hurting and needy children and adults of all races and cultures. LAIC helps to solve the moral decay, crime, drug, gang, homelessness, and poverty epidemic that exists in America's cities.

The compassion of Jesus is seen throughout all aspects of the Dream Center ministry. Hope comes to children, teenagers and adults as physical needs are met and spiritual needs are addressed simultaneously. Team members use exciting, relevant outreaches to make contact with people. Heartache and destruction are replaced by hope and opportunity.

Serving as the model in over one hundred cities, the L.A. Dream Center now joins with churches and individuals of all denominations around the world to meet the spiritual and socioeconomic needs of the inner city.

A Day in the Life of the International Dream Center

- Prayer is offered by clusters of ministry teams.

- Disciples who have come out of impoverished neighborhoods are commissioned to return and be Jesus to their neighbors.

- A call for salvation goes out to a group of street people who have gathered to receive food and listen to a story from the Bible.

- A team of three fans out incognito (in sun glasses) to speak to as many as possible up and down Sunset Boulevard, many who live their lives in an ocean of sin.

- A free concert offers Rap, Blues and Rock with complimentary food and drinks to bait some youth into hearing about Jesus.

- A group of workers fishes among children and their parents at an inner city playground.

- Hundreds come for food and a blanket and learn about a hope they could dare believe for.

- Study groups develop working relationships with converts through spiritual growth.

- Adult students take GED classes and others find vocational training that will deliver them from welfare.

- Former addicts are cleaning the residences of those in the full-time discipleship program as a work/study program.

The list could go on, but the message is clear. The international Dream Center provides turning points for individuals who live in L.A. The compassion of Jesus extends from first-contact through to graduation for active mission duty. And through this a dream finds its destiny.[3]

Compassionate Christianity—Seeking Our Brothers

SERVING THE POOR OF THE WORLD

Mother Teresa and the Missionaries of Charity

She was born Agnes Gonxha Bojaxhiu in 1910 in Skopje, Yugoslavia (now Macedonia). In 1928 she decided to become a nun and went to Dublin, Ireland, to join the Sisters of Loreto. From there she went to the Loreto convent in Darjeeling, India.

In 1929 she began to teach geography at St. Mary's High School for Girls in Calcutta. In those days the streets of Calcutta were crowded with beggars, lepers, and the homeless. Unwanted infants were regularly abandoned on the streets or in garbage bins. In 1946, Mother Teresa felt the need to abandon her teaching position to care for the needy in the slums of Calcutta.

Initially focusing her efforts on poor children in the streets, Mother Teresa taught them how to read and how to care for themselves. Many former students of St. Mary's eventually joined her order. Each girl who joined was required to devote her life to serving the poor without accepting any material reward in return.[4]

Here are a few selections from the Angel of Mercy, Mother Teresa.

When I pick up a person from the street, hungry, I give him a plate of rice, a piece of bread. But a person who is shut out, who feels unwanted, unloved, terrified, the person who has been thrown out of society - that spiritual poverty is much harder to overcome.

Those who are materially poor can be very wonderful people. One evening we went out and we picked up four people from the street. And one of them was in a most terrible condition. I told the Sisters:

"You take care of the other three; I will take care of the one who looks worse."

So I did for her all that my love can do. I put her in bed, and there was such a beautiful smile on her face. She took hold of my hand, as she said one word only:

"Thank you" - and she died.

I could not help but examine my conscience before her. And I asked: "What would I say if I were in her place?" And my answer was very simple. I would have tried to draw a little attention to myself. I would have said: "I am hungry, I am dying, I am cold, I am in pain," or something. But she gave me much more, she gave me her grateful love.

And she died with a smile on her face.

Then there was the man we picked up from the drain, half eaten by worms and, after we had brought him to the home, he only said, "I have lived like an animal in the street, but I am going to die as an angel, loved and cared for." Then, after we had removed all the worms from his body, all he said, with a big smile, was: "Sister, I am going home to God" - and he died. It was so wonderful to see the greatness of that man who could speak like that without blaming anybody, without comparing anything.

Like an angel - this is the greatness of people who are spiritually rich even when they are materially poor....
"Life"
Life is an opportunity, benefit from it.
Life is beauty, admire it.
Life is bliss, taste it.
Life is a dream, realise it.
Life is a challenge, meet it.
Life is a duty, complete it.
Life is a game, play it.
Life is costly, care for it.
Life is wealth, keep it.

Life is love, enjoy it.
Life is mystery, know it.
Life is a promise, fulfil it.
Life is sorrow, overcome it.
Life is a song, sing it.
Life is a struggle, accept it.
Life is tragedy, confront it.
Life is an adventure, dare it.
Life is luck, make it.
Life is too precious, do not destroy it.
Life is life, fight for it.[5]

Demonstrating God's Love

OPERATION BLESSING INTERNATIONAL

The mission of Operation Blessing International is to demonstrate God's love by alleviating human need and suffering in the United States and around the world....

In efforts to relieve human suffering, we combat hunger, deprivation and physical affliction with the provision of food, clothing, shelter, medical care and other basic necessities of life. We also help facilitate the development of healthy, vibrant, and self-sustaining communities by addressing larger issues of education, food security, potable water, employment, community health, and disaster mitigation projects. In every endeavor, OBI seeks to exemplify Christian compassion and benevolence while conforming to the highest standards of integrity....

Founded on November 14, 1978 by religious broadcaster, businessman and philanthropist, Pat Robertson, Operation Blessing was originally set up to help struggling individuals and families by matching their needs for items such as clothing, appliances, vehicles with donated items from viewers of the 700 Club....

Operation Blessing's impact increased dramatically when local churches and helping organizations agreed to provide matching funds for assistance projects and individual aid...Special types of needs led to additional projects, such as an annual distribution of thousand of blankets to the homeless and a program that provides seeds for community vegetable gardens....

While Operation Blessing's outreach was spreading throughout the United States, commitment to helping hungry people and disaster victims in foreign lands was also growing....By its 10th anniversary, Operation Blessing had spent $40 million of its own funds worldwide and through the cooperation of other organizations, had leveraged that amount to approximately $196 million....

In 1994, Operation Blessing also introduced the Convoy of Hope concept, which through partnerships with churches and other ministries nationwide, has developed into an effective relief assistance and evangelistic outreach which serves tens of thousands of people each year.

OBI's medical missions, which provide medical relief in underserved countries, undertook its first mission in 1994. The program sends volunteer teams of doctors, dentists, other health care professionals and support staff on one to two week missions.... OBI commissioned The Flying Hospital, a specially equipped L1011 jet aircraft...[which] provides facilities for world-class medical/surgical services to people in developing countries and disaster-stricken areas....

Operation Blessing developed a mutual partnership with the Outreach Foundation (OF) to expand and enhance OF's WINGS Life Skills Training, a 40-hour life skills training course designed to help the chronically unemployed and underemployed successfully transition into the workforce....

"The mission of Operation Blessing International is simple," says Pat Robertson, who serves as OBI's chairman of the board. "Its purpose is to help people who cannot help themselves. One of the cornerstones of our Christian faith is to serve others. That's what Operation Blessing International is all about."[6]

Making a Lasting Difference in a World of Need

MERCY SHIPS

Does this sound like a set of values that you would ascribe to?

We love God.

We love and serve people.

We are people of integrity.

We are committed to excellence in all we do.

These may be broad-sweeping but put in context of the ministry of the Mercy Ships, these are striking contrasts many governments of the countries in which they serve. Mercy Ships brings hope and healing to the poor and needy around the world, primarily through ocean-going vessels, providing medical care, relief, development, and education. It is Mercy Ships' goal to serve one million people annually by the year 2004.

This mission agency populates a fleet of ships with doctors, water engineers, teachers, and agriculturists able to visit some of the world's poorest cities. These crew members serve from two weeks to a lifetime. Each share a common desire to help the poor and hopeless around the world. These crews bring life-changing services, food, medicines, and skills free of charge. The Mercy Ships have completed projects in more than 70 ports around the world bringing immediate relief to tens of thousands and long-term sustainable change to each port in which they drop anchor.

Mercy Ships operates the largest non-governmental hospital ship in the world, the Anastasis. Since its inception in 1978, Mercy Ships has performed 8,000 onboard operations, treated more than 200,000 people in village medical clinics, performed 100,000 dental treatments, taught local health care workers, provided tens of millions of dollars of medical equipment, hospital supplies, and medicines, and completed more than 250 construction and agricultural projects.

The lasting effects of Mercy Ships are recognized by leaders around the globe. When one considers the magnitude of the suffering in the world, it is easy to become overwhelmed into complacency or despair. Mercy Ships does what is within its means to touch as many hurting, bruised, and crushed lives as possible. And they do it just as Jesus did...one by one.[7]

Hope, Compassion and Justice

PRISON FELLOWSHIP MINISTRIES

If one wants to name some of the most unlovely sort of human beings, the mind will think of those in prisons. Jesus was arrested; Paul spent time behind bars; Peter knew what it meant to be imprisoned. These three may seem more the exception than the rule, but Jesus asks us to free the captives. If not in the literal sense, at least their souls and spirits can come into a glorious liberty.

Prison Fellowship Ministries has captured the unlikely task of ministering to those who, guilty or not, find themselves incarcerated. Their volunteers bring hope and compassion to prisoners, sharing the gospel of Jesus Christ as they do so. Most have heard of founder Chuck Colson, who has firsthand experience as to how prison life can affect the inner being as well as the outer circumstances of a life and a family. Each aspect of the ministry reflects the mission of Prison Fellowship: to exhort, equip, and assist the Church in its ministry to prisoners, ex-prisoners, victims, and their families, and to promote biblical standards of justice in the criminal justice system.

There are many simple ways to touch a prisoner's life. Prayer Ministry lifts specific needs and petitions in unified prayer; Write a Prisoner give opportunities for people to become pen pals with those behind bars; In-Prison Ministry trains those who enter prison doors to hold Bible Studies or mentor prisoners one-on-one. The popular Angel Tree program addresses the need for prisoners' children to be touched through Christmas gifts and camp sponsorships.

Most Americans are fearful of crime and frustrated by the current justice system, noting that nothing has seemed to work in breaking the cycle of crime. A strong force that makes a difference in many lives is a branch of Prison Ministries called Justice Fellowship. This public policy organization is dedicated to advancing the Biblically based restorative justice principle throughout the United States. Justice Fellowship provides research, trains volunteers, and is an advocate for restorative programs at every level of the criminal justice system. It has become a leading voice for change in the capital of the nation as well as most states.

Although at first glance it may seem that this ministry is more political than Christian, one only has to hear the heart cry of the current president, Pat Nolan, to sense the compassion of Jesus. "Justice Fellowship...works to spread the good news about Restorative Justice: biblically based, common-sense reforms of our criminal justice system that heal victims, hold offenders accountable, reconcile victims and offenders, and restore peace to our communities."[8]

Hope Changes Everything

WORLD VISION

What began as one man's vision of a world without hunger, disease, and hopelessness, has grown into the world's largest Christian international relief and development agency—World Vision.

Founded in 1950 by Dr. Bob Pierce to help children orphaned in the Korean War, World Vision has grown well beyond its child-assistance roots to facilitating the transformation of entire communities with water programs, health care education, agricultural and economic development, and strategic Christian leadership activities. During [its 50th anniversary in 2000], World Vision served well over 50 million people in 103 countries, including the United States.[9]

World Vision is a Christian organization, yet it does not limit its mission to Christians alone. Its services are offered freely regardless of belief, ethnic background, or gender. World Vision deals in practical issues but casts a vision in its recipients to see the fulfillment of their dream of self-sufficiency. Each WV worker represents Jesus

Christ's love and compassion for people impacted by war, poverty or disaster.

World Vision is an international partnership of Christians whose mission is to follow our Lord and Savior Jesus Christ in working with the poor and oppressed to promote human transformation, seek justice, and bear witness to the good news of the kingdom of God. The agency pursues this mission through integrated, holistic commitment to:

- transformational development that is community-based and sustainable, focused especially on the needs of children;

- emergency relief that assists people afflicted by conflict or disaster;

- promotion of justice that seeks to change unjust structures affecting the poor among whom we work;

- strategic initiatives that serve the Church in the fulfillment of its mission;

- public awareness that leads to informed understanding, giving, involvement, and prayer;

- witness to Jesus Christ by life, deed, word, and signs that encourage people to respond to the Gospel.[10]

WV puts forth an annual listing of the world's ten most violent and vulnerable areas. Unlike many, who would shrink back from these volatile "global hot spots," World Vision breaks new ground and seeks these nations or regions out. The agency is quick to respond to send relief in the form of food, clothing and medical supplies, but also hastens to send workers who will care for the people both physically and spiritually.

Children are central to World Vision's ministry, because Jesus is clear on the treatment of children. "If anyone causes one of these little ones who believe in Me to sin, it would be better for him to have a large millstone hung around his neck and to be drowned in the depths of the sea" (Mt. 18:6 NIV). Children are being used and abused in shameful ways in large numbers around the world. Many are literally fighting for their lives. World Vision offers a sponsorship program where individuals can help rescue a child from exploitation and despair.

World Vision is headquartered in Washington state, near Seattle. Through links to government agencies and members of Congress, World Vision is one of the first called upon to render aid when an emergency situation creates casualties. This ministry is truly a testimony of Christ's compassion for mankind.[11]

A Revolution in Compassion

WE CARE AMERICA

There are a multitude of compassion ministries within America, yet We Care America is not just simply one of the many. In order to meet the needs of compassion within the United States, "faith-based, corporate, and civic sectors need to be brought together to empower the poor to become mature Christians, good parents, and productive citizens. The timing is even more critical as millions of Americans reach their five-year lifetime limit on welfare assistance....

We Care America's mission is to identify faith-based programs that provide *proven* practical and spiritual help to these people....

We Care America's mission is therefore to *unify, equip,* and *enable* existing organizations, so they can accomplish their mission even more efficiently."[12]

The following are some examples of the programs We Care America is working with churches and faith-based organizations to replicate:

- *After-school programs* that rescue at-risk children...

- *Care ministries* that equip lay leaders to respond to the pastoral needs of their church...

- *Welfare to work programs*...

- *Disaster response strategies…*

- *Supply networks* that connect food banks and missions to exchange resources…

- *Drug and alcohol prevention* and recovery programs…

- *Discipleship…*for new Christians…[13]

Dave Donaldson, We Care America's CEO, leads his team in making the Martha work in America more efficient and more effective. WCA draws groups from different streams together so they can benefit from the experience of the others. They are networked with potential sources of funds and volunteers. Those who participate receive information vital to their ministry of compassion. The team works with communities so that local branches of national ministries and agencies connect to address certain projects.

WCA works closely with the government as it enlists faith-based organizations to combat social problems. We Care America facilitated the meeting between top Christian leaders and the Office of Faith-Based and Community initiatives (OFBCI). This meeting (May 31, 2001) represented a broad cross-section of Christian leaders of all ethnic, political and denomination backgrounds. Future gatherings will encompass business leaders and ministry practicioners.[14]

Compassion for Those on the Outer Fringes of Society

TEEN CHALLENGE

"Teen Challenge is the oldest, largest and most successful program of its kind in the world. Established in 1958 by David Wilkerson, Teen Challenge has grown to more than 150 centers in the United States and 250 centers world-wide."[15] The story of how Teen Challenge started is told in the book *The Cross and the Switchblade*, which was also made into a movie starring Pat Boone.

Teen Challenge offers a number of services to the community, many times free of charge. For over 40 years, Teen Challenge has been going into schools around the world working with teens to educate them about the dangers of drugs. Our school teams consist of 8-10 Teen Challenge residents and a staff member. These are men and women who once had problems with drugs, so they know what they are talking about when they talk to teens. For younger children we have a puppet show that we use to educate them in a way that they can easily understand. Our presentations usually run from 45 minutes to an hour in length. Any school or Boy/Girl scout troop that is interested in scheduling a visit should contact the nearest Teen Challenge center.

Teen Challenge reaches out to people in juvenile halls, jails, and prisons. Our "jail teams" help show inmates that there is hope for them to turn their lives around. And more importantly, we educate them in how to change their lives!

Turning Point Meetings

Many of our centers hold weekly support group meetings such as Turning Point. Turning Point's purpose is to assist the local church establish an effective, on-going, biblically-based, small group ministry to help people overcome and/or remain free of life-controlling problems. Turning Point groups are designed to have a beginning and an end. Some support groups never have an end, and this can wear your staff down as well as make people too dependent on a narrow group of people. Turning Point groups are designed to last nine to thirteen weeks. The desire is to apply the truths of Scripture to the struggles that we face in order that we may grow in our relationship to God and experience growing freedom from the "corruption in the world caused by evil desires" (II Peter 1:4 NIV)....

Residential Programs

Many of our centers offer a one-year residential program for adults designed to help men and women learn how to live drug-free lives. During their 1-year stay, they do not hold down outside jobs, as all of their attention is focused on the program. We challenge the residents to embrace the Christian faith. We see that when they do, their lives are transformed and they find true meaning and purpose.

Residents follow strict rules and discipline. All residents adhere to a daily schedule which includes chapel, Bible classes and work assignments on or near the grounds....

While most of our centers are for adults, some do offer residential programs for teenagers. Please contact the Teen Challenge center nearest you to find out what services they offer.

How does one get into the Teen Challenge residential program?

The number one question people ask us is how to get someone into the residential program or to get them involved with the other services Teen Challenge offers.

The procedure for getting in the Teen Challenge program varies from center to center. Some of our centers house teens only, while many of our other centers are for adult men or women only....

In general, you will first call and setup an interview. The interview serves two purposes. It allows the induction personnel to explain the program to the prospective individual and what is expected of a resident in the program.

For the other services Teen Challenge has to offer such as school presentations, counseling, and weekly meetings, check our "Directory of Teen Challenge centers page" [on the website] and contact the center nearest you to find out the specific services they have to offer.

Studes have shown a 70-80 percent cure rate for Teen Challenge graduates.

Since Teen Challenge first opened its doors to drug addicts and alcoholics in 1958, thousands have come seeking help. Two significant research projects have confirmed the effectiveness of the Teen Challenge approach to helping those affected by life-controlling problems. Researchers credit the spiritual component of the program as the key to the high success rate of Teen Challenge graduates.[16]

Getting Relief to the World

CONVOY OF HOPE

Convoy of Hope provides resources to local organizations to meet physical and spiritual needs for the purpose of making communities a better place. It serves in the United States and around the world providing disaster relief, building supply lines and sponsoring outreaches to the poor and hurting in communities. During a COH outreach, free groceries are distributed, job and health fairs are organized and activities for children are provided.

Some features of Convoy of Hope are:

- 300,000 square-feet distribution center

- Fleet of 18-wheeler semi-trucks

- Experienced logistics team

- Ability to gather resources from across the nation

- Distributes food across America and around the world

- Conducts events in approximately 30 cities and 10 countries each year

- Partners with government, businesses and non-profit organizations to build community unity

    The partnership between businesses, suppliers and Convoy of Hope has resulted in many families receiving help. Together we have accomplished the following:

- Distributed more than 20 million pounds of food to needy families in the United States and around the world

- Provided food to more that 2 million people

- Placed shelters, water purification units and other supplies around the world

- Responded to disasters and crises in 30 countries

- Mobilized more than 100,000 volunteers and over 5,000 organizations to offer assistance to families in need[17]

Reaching Your Own Community

LIGHTHOUSE MOVEMENT

The Lighthouse Movement is the major evangelism initiative of the Mission America Coalition. A Lighthouse is one or more Christians gathered in Jesus' name, committing to pray for, care for and share Jesus Christ with their neighbors, family and friends who don't know Him. The Coalition's prayerful goal is for at least 30,000 local churches to become Lighthouse Churches and at least 3,000,000 individual Christians to become Lighthouses to pray, care and share with every person in their area. Already, Coalition partners have already established an estimated 8,000 Lighthouse Churches and nearly 1 million individual Lighthouses.

Some of the ministries involved with the Lighthouse Movement are: Aglow International, African Methodist Episcopal Zion Church, Alpha North America, American Bible Society, American Baptist Churches, American Tract Society, American Family Association, Assemblies of God, International Fellowship Association of Vineyard Churches, Awana Clubs International, Bethany Fellowship International, Billy Graham Center, Bob Weiner Ministries, Caleb Project, Campus Crusade for Christ, Christian Broadcasting Network Inc., Elim Fellowship, Intercessors for America, Pray! Magazine, Regent University, The Salvation Army, and hundreds of others.

Mission America's Lighthouse Movement is providing a rallying point for Christians in the new millennium. The Coalition provides published information, consultations, seminars and [a] website to help Christians learn more about being a Lighthouse and then to find resources to assist them to pray with God's love, care with God's strength and share with God's power.[18]

In recent months it has become apparent that God is expanding The Lighthouse Movement internationally. Contacts are coming almost daily from Christians in Japan, South America, Africa,

Europe, etc. who are interested in establishing The Lighthouse Movement in their own country. Interestingly, recent contact has come from American Christians working abroad who are sensing God's call to become Lighthouses.

Opportunites for Involvement

You can be a part of The Lighthouse Movement! Join thousands of other Christians who are pushing back the darkness in their neighborhoods and communities and are sharing the love and grace of God.

Begin today by praying for a few friends, neighbors or co-workers who don't know Jesus Christ. As you pray for them, look for opportunities to care for them - showing the love of Jesus through acts of kindness and building friendships. Then as you care for them, God will open doors for you to share your faith with them through a personal witness or maybe an invitation to an outreach event in your church.

Many of the Mission America/Lighthouse Movement partners have developed wonderful resources to help you be an effective Lighthouse – reflecting the Light of Jesus Christ....

Is God calling your Church to take responsibility for reaching people in your neighborhood? The involvement of you and your church is crucial. Local pastors and churches are key to helping equip and sustain individual Lighthouses. And, as God blesses the ministry of each Lighthouse, a strong connection with a local church is essential for the follow-up and discipleship of new converts.

A Key Lighthouse Church:

1. Models a dynamic Lighthouse congregation.

2. Mobilizes two or three other churches to participate in their area.

3. Monitors the progress of the community effort to make sure all areas and all groups are reached with prayer and the Gospel.

If one church in each of the 28,500 five-digit Zip Codes in America mobilizes two or three other churches in their area to become Lighthouse Churches - this effort will effectively cover our entire nation with prayer and the Gospel! No one person, church, denomination or ministry can hope to reach our nation alone. It's only when we work together, setting aside our differences that our nation will truly be impacted by prayer and evangelism. Now is the time to be involved in a unified effort to reach our country - neighborhood by neighborhood.

Here are some great ways to reach out to your community:

Ideas for Caring

We've put together some simple ideas on how to begin caring for your neighbors. Some of these ideas take a little planning while others are a matter of becoming aware of opportunities to show you care:

- Meet new (just moved in) neighbors with a plate of cookies, a warm welcome and a 3X5 card with your name, address and phone number. Suggest they call you with any questions about the neighborhood such as garbage collection, shopping, post office, etc.

- Put together a neighborhood directory of names, addresses and phone numbers. This helps you pray more specifically for your neighbors and assists everyone in getting to know each other.

- Take dinner to new parents. Use disposable containers so the clean up is quick and easy. Plan a neighborhood baby shower for a new baby. Invite several neighbors to assist you.

- Baby-sit for your neighbors. In many cases, families don't have grandparents or relatives in the area who might be able to help. Many young parents rarely have extra time or money to go on a "date." Make sure they - and you - are comfortable with the arrangements and that you know how to contact them should an emergency arise. Can you organize a baby-sitting co-op?

- Call on housebound neighbors. They might enjoy a personal visit or may just want to talk with you on the telephone. If you do visit, take a little something such as a dessert, fruit or a book.

- If you have children or grandchildren, consider taking them with you when you visit housebound neighbors. What joy for an older person to just see and watch the children play! Or if the children visit you, let the neighbor know they're welcome to come over and "play."

- Do your neighbors love to read? Consider buying an extra copy of a good Christian novel and sharing it with them. Or, as you finish the books you're reading, start a "lending library" to your neighbors....

- Take a spaghetti dinner to someone recuperating from surgery. Include a simple garden bouquet and a get-well card.

- Plan "spur of the moment" or next day coffee/tea or lemonade times and invite two to four neighbors to get better acquainted....

- Does it get windy in your area? When the wind blows, take the time to pick up trash off neighbors' lawns and garbage cans that have blown all over. They'll learn who rescues their garbage cans and recyclable containers. You may get a reputation for being the helpful neighbor!

- When you're baking, consider preparing a few extra cupcakes, cookies, pies, etc. Save them to give to a neighbor the Lord may lay on your heart....

- Learn people's names, as well as the names of their children and pets. Don't be snoopy, but try to notice a new car or a new hairstyle, etc. People love to be given an honest compliment, even about the new tree they planted in their front yard. Change your walking or exercising schedule if needed, to walk with a neighbor. As you're walking, listen to them. It's probably one of the greatest ways to serve a neighbor or friend.

- Begin a Neighborhood Bible Study. Invite the neighbors who are most interested over for dinner as an introduction....

- Host a neighborhood BBQ or block party along with one or two other families in the area. Choose a special holiday time or theme for the party.[19]

God in the Marketplace

REACHING MEN IN THE BUSINESS WORLD
FULL GOSPEL BUSINESS MEN'S FELLOWSHIP

The Full Gospel Business Men's Fellowship is the largest network of Christian businessmen in the world. From every part of the world - 160 nations. Every race, color, culture and almost every language - we include: Kings, Presidents, Prime Ministers, former Presidents, Senators, Members of Parliament, Generals, Judges, Captains of Industry, businessmen, executives professionals, sales and office workers, factory workers, educators and young people just getting started.

The Full Gospel Business Men's Fellowship International is an organization sovereignly ordained by God. From its humble beginnings - one small chapter in Los Angeles, California 1951 - it was thrust into global ministry by prophetic visions and prophecy. The Fellowship's story graphically depicts man's plans falling short of the mark, but God's plan succeeding. The complete story is in the classic inspirational book, The Happiest People on Earth, by Demos Shakarian, the California dairyman who is the Fellowship's founder. The book is co-authored by the celebrated Christian writers John and Elizabeth Sherrill.

Today the Fellowship operates in 132 countries. Thousands of chapters hold meetings in small hamlets, farm towns, outlying suburbs and urban power centers. Breakfast, lunch and dinner, these meetings are a time of fellowship, outreach and personal ministry.

But the backbone of the fellowship is its men - men who have a vision inspired by God to reach out beyond their personal lives - to help others find the reality of the Spirit-filled walk with Christ

- ten of thousands of men putting God first and letting their lights shine to the world - men who join the Fellowship and participate in the ministry outreaches available, making a commitment to spread the Good News of Christ through the effective and powerful worldwide ministries of the Full Gospel Business Men's Fellowship International.

Our vision for the fellowship is based upon a series of prophetic messages given over a period of time and confirmed by a literal vision from God.

In the vision, untold masses of men from every continent and nation, of all races and diverse culture and costume, once spiritually dead, are now alive. Delivered and set free, they are filled with power of God's Holy Spirit, faces radiant with glory, hands raised and voice lifting their praises to heaven.

We see a vast global movement of laymen being used mightily by God to bring in this last great harvest through the outpouring of God's Holy Spirit before the return of our Lord Jesus Christ.

Our mission statement

- To call men back to God.

-To help believers to be baptized in the Holy Spirit and to grow spiritually.

-To train and equip men to fulfill the Great Commission

-To provide an opportunity for Christian fellowship

-To bring greater unity among all people in the body of Christ.[20]

Chaplains in the Business World

MARKETPLACE MINISTRIES

Marketplace Ministries is a faith-based, proactive and personalized Employee Assistance Provider. Client companies receive a team of chaplains who visit the work site weekly and are available for crisis care and pastoral activities 24 hours-a-day, 365 days-a-year. Chaplains help meet the needs of company employees and their families under an umbrella of compassion and concern.

Based in Dallas, Texas, Marketplace Ministries has expanded in the last 18 years into 34 states and 329 cities. Client companies with multiple locations are able to have chaplain teams at each of their sites. Additionally, through a nationwide network of on-call chaplains, Marketplace Ministries is able to care for employees and family members anywhere in the United States.

We take care of a company's most important asset: employees and their families. Our Employee Assistance Program reaps many benefits for the client company as our trained chaplains offer work site relationships, pastoral care ministries, crisis care, and company support activities. Increased loyalty to the company, reduction in absenteeism, enhanced appreciation for management, increased productivity, and reduction in employee turnover are just a few of the many dividends a company can receive by partnering with Marketplace Ministries....

As we provide our program, it offers the optimum opportunity for ministry of service available today. The provision of a team of chaplains who are trained and experienced, neutral from the company structure, totally confidential in all conversations with employees and are available 24 hours-a-day, 365 days-a-year is a company benefit without equal. The chaplain team is able to extend the personal interest, care and concern of company leadership while allowing those leaders to devote their time and energy to running the company. We represent an extension of their compassion for those on their staff. For those in the work force who are "disconnected and misdirected," the chaplain represents a resource for help they would not otherwise have. Our opportunities to impact the lives of people with eternal significance, and our chance to minister to people at work, are frequent.[21]

Training Leaders for the Workplace

MARKETPLACE LEADERS

There is a move of God taking place in the workplace today. Will you be a part of it?

God is touching the hearts of men and women in the workplace today. Grassroots organizations have begun around the country. Ten years ago we could only identify 25 formalized marketplace ministries. Today, we have identified over 900 and this list is growing all the time.

Men and women are hungering for more than just material success. But how do we respond to this hunger and help men and women understand how to translate this into a lifestyle? That is why Marketplace Leaders was established.

Marketplace Leader's purpose is to raise up and train men and women to fulfill their calling in and through the workplace and to view their work as their ministry.

Our primary means of accomplishing this is through four key focuses:

1. Building Unity (John 17:23)

Among marketplace ministry organizations which includes bringing leaders together at Marketplace Leader Summits. In addition, we publish several email publications for leaders such as the Marketplace Resource Connection, a monthly report on the activity and resources of marketplace ministries.

2. Training New Leaders

Raising up new leaders through mentoring and training programs such as the Called to the Workplace workshops is just one such training workshop provided by Marketplace Leaders. Here you will discover what God says about work, calling and adversity....

3. Publishing

Currently Marketplace Leaders publishes three newsletters: Marketplace Meditations (daily), Marketplace Rhema (monthly) and Resource Connection (monthly)....Our online Catalog consist of specially selected books for the marketplace Christian designed to give you a selection of books that will encourage you to go deeper with Christ....

4. Consulting

Does your business or ministry need assistance in strategic planning or creative services? We've had over twenty years of working with Christian and secular companies in assisting them with their marketing communications needs.[22]

Mission in the World—Going to the Nations

To Know God and Make Him Known

YOUTH WITH A MISSION

Imagine a group of group of young people who sign up for an adventure of a lifetime. They are given a two-pronged approach to relevant Christianity. They are intensely discipled in the ways of God and the disciplines that draw men closer to Him, yet they are also thrust into domestic and international mission work to work out the "Great Commission" and put their discipleship to the test. This is not a dream, it is reality for 12,000 volunteer staff based in over 700 locations in over 135 countries, one of the largest interdenominational and international Christian ministries in existence today. This is...Youth With A Mission.

"Words Plus Action" are the bywords of those who participate in this ministry. Youth With A Mission (YWAM) opportunities vary widely and cover everything from A to Z. Each project and event helps form one of the three main strands which weave together the mission of YWAM: training and education, mercy ministries, and evangelism and frontier missions.

Training and education within the Youth With A Mission ministry offers a degree program through the University of the Nations, where individuals are able to specialize in areas of science, technology, communications, humanities and Christian ministry. The basic training for all YWAMers is Discipleship Training School, the prerequisite to all other training programs.

Mercy Ministries may look like a typical compassion agency on the outside, but it doesn't take long to find its impact so extensive that it meets practical and physical needs of over 400,000 people annually. This mercy comes in such varied forms that it would take a dictionary to cover all of them. But the Good News is declared through every helping hand that is extended.

Evangelism and Frontier Ministries are integral to training Christians as YWAM offers skill-building in the creative arts that are used as tools to reach a wide audience. Church-planting is a cooperative effort between YWAM and denominations and local churches. Frontier missions involve outreach to "classical" remote mission fields, as well as vast, needy urban centers.

Youth With A Mission provides useful tools for all who would pray for the world with an informed mind. *Operation World*, provides a prayer and reference handbook that outlines each country with facts and points of intercession. The *Personal Prayer Diary Planner* places an informative journal into the hands of those who need such. YWAM's World is as large as the globe and as close as your own devotional time. But that is why they exist: *to know God and make Him known.*[23]

Revolutionizing a Generation With the Gospel

TEEN MANIA

In 1986 Teen Mania Ministries was founded in Tulsa, Oklahoma by Ron and Katie Luce. The next summer, 60 teenagers went on Teen Mania's first mission trip to Guatemala. In the fall of 1988, the Teen Mania Honor Academy internship program began with its first class of six participants.

Teen Mania's Acquire The Fire started in the fall of 1991. Since its inception, over one million guests have attended a weekend ATF youth event in one of 32 major cities around the country. Teen Mania launched its first dome event, "Day One," at the Silverdome in Pontiac, Michigan in 1999 with 70,000 in attendance. Teen Mania hosted two other dome events, "Stand-UP!" at the Silverdome in 2000 and "Stand-UP!" Florida at Tropicana Field in St. Petersburg, Florida in 2001. One out of every 48 teenagers in the state of Florida attended.

Teen Mania has one of the busiest web sites in the world for teenagers and sponsors a daily on-line devotional site with over 50,000 registered users. Teen Mania also hosts a weekly television program, Acquire the Fire, shown in 1800 outlets around the globe. Since its beginning, Teen Mania's Global Expeditions has sent 32,710 teens onto mission fields in 50 different countries. Here are some of the opportunities with Teen Mania:

Acquire the Fire

The guiding purpose of Acquire the Fire over the past 10 years has been to train teenagers to have a "Relentless Pursuit of God" and a "Relentless Pursuit of the People He Loves." Each year, Acquire the Fire hosts weekend youth events featuring top Christian speakers and music artists in a powerful presentation packed with pyrotechnics, drama, and cutting edge video. ATF now hosts stadium events each year in addition to the Acquire the Fire youth events.

Global Expeditions

Utilizing teenagers for global missions is a key strategy of Teen Mania's ministry. Over the years, Global Expeditions has experienced immense growth. Each summer and Christmas break, Teen Mania takes thousands of teenagers on mission trips around the world. In the summer of 2001, 5,120 teenagers went to 29 countries worldwide. Teen Mania has witnessed over 1,000,000 nationals give their lives to Christ through Global Expeditions.

Honor Academy

The Honor Academy is one solid year of fast-paced, life-and-leadership training, designed to be spiritually maturing, academically challenging, and physically intense. Honor Academy participants are developed in five highlighted areas of Spiritual Growth, Professional Excellence, Intellectual Development, Emotional Maturity, and Physical Fitness. The internship program started in 1988 with only a handful of participants. Over the years, the program has grown tremendously and at present there are over 700 Honor Academy participants.[24]

Reflective questions and spiritual exercises

CONTEMPORARY PORTRAITS OF COMPASSIONATE CHRISTIANITY

And the beat goes on...

This chapter plays a compassionate song of cultural diversity. In their own genre, each ministry plays its tune to a different audience, with different instruments, using the same maestro—The Holy Spirit. Our lyric is "hope" and our melody is "love." The love of Jesus drives the people who orchestrate the outreaches described in this chapter to extreme measures. This is not fiction or fantasy! We need to find our place in this symphony of compassion.

REFLECTIONS AND RECIPES

1.   Create your own recipe: "Love's Fragrance."
                Mix together
                        Radiating Christ's holiness
                        Joy of Jesus as your strength
                        Be happy
                        Be at peace
                        Accept and give all with a smile

Rate yourself on the above ingredients. Does your love have a beautiful fragrance or could it be improved? How can you make the necessary improvements so that you can do as Mother Teresa and spread the fragrance of love everywhere you go?

2.   Explain how you can tell between the fragrance of genuine love and pseudo-love's manipulation and control. How do people respond to the "love" you give them? Do they perceive it to be genuine? Have they accused you of manipulation or control? Examine your motives. Have you had agendas that shadow the purity of love and taint its expression? Confession, repentance and restoration are necessary to release you from any stronghold. Take time to go through this process and experience the victory that is awaiting you.

3.   Has there been an expression of genuine love that was not recognized as such, even though it was given sincerely from your heart? How does the communication of love have as much weight as the heart's desire to

love? How can you learn to communicate your intentions so that others will understand and receive in a greater way?

4.   When Mary anointed Jesus with the costly oil,"...the house was filled with the fragrance of the oil" (Jn. 12:3). The fragrance that Jesus received was of the love Mary had, even more than the spikenard's pungent aroma. For us to spread the love of Jesus everywhere we go, we first have to experience it. Write a paragraph about the love God has for you and how He expresses it to you.

5.   "In her own way, Martha was a passionate God Chaser, too. No one goes to the trouble Martha did just to offer a 'home away from home' to a traveling preacher" (*Chasing God, Serving Man*, 48). Today is pregnant with possibilities. No matter how many meetings or activities you have ahead of you, you have every opportunity to spread the fragrance of love everywhere you go. But you must "Chase God" first and receive the love in order to give it away. Take time before you begin your day to love on God and let Him love you. Then get ready for a truly incredible adventure!

ENDNOTES

1. Bart Pierce, *Seeking Our Brothers* (Shippensburg, PA: Fresh Bread, 2000), pp. 77-80. Used by permission.

2. Ibid, pp. 67-69.

3. www.dreamcenter.org Used by permission. Reprinted as is.

4. Donald L. Milam, Jr., *The Lost Passions of Jesus* (Shippensburg, PA: Mercy-Place, 1999), p. 131. Used by permission.

5. Home1.pacific.net.sg/~alquek/teresa1.htm Used by permission. Reprinted as is.

6. www.ob.org Used by permission. Reprinted as is.

7. www.mercyships.com/sitemap.shtml Used by permission.

8. www.christianity.com/prisonfellowship Used by permission.

9. www.worldvision.org Used by permission.

10. Ibid.

11. Ibid.

12. www.wecareamerica.org Used by permission.

13. Ibid.

14. Ibid.

15. www.teenchallenge.com Used by permission.

16. Ibid. Used by permission. Reprinted as is.

17. www.convoyofhope.org Used by permission. Reprinted as is.

18. www.lighthousemovement.com Used by permission. Reprinted as is.

19. Ibid.

20. www.fgbmfi.org Used by permission. Reprinted as is.

21. www.marketplaceministries.com Used by permission.
22. www.marketplaceleaders.org Used by permission. Reprinted as is.
23. www.ywam.org Used by permission.
24. www.teenmania.com Used by permission. Reprinted as is.

Section III

RESOURCES

Chapter Seven

Resources for the Compassionate God Chaser

We have reached the end, but the book would not be complete if I did not leave you with a resource list that would help you to contact others who will enhance your personal pursuit and help you to develop your own private recipes for compassionate service.

First, I would like to give you the information for contacting my own ministry, GodChasers.network. I am above all a God chaser, but I do appreciate and support those serving the needs of man. In many ways I am a bridge builder. I love creating networks that bridge the gap between those ministries involved in passionate pursuit and compassionate ministry.

This is only a partial list of the hundreds of thousands of ministries that are on the front lines of service. It will serve you as a resource at many times, depending on what season of life you find yourself in.

GodChasers.Network
Post Office Box 3355
Pineville, Louisiana 71361

Devotional Books for the Passionate God Chaser

Tommy Tenney

God Chasers (Shippensburg, PA: Destiny Image, 1998)
God Catchers (Nashville, TN: Thomas Nelson, 2001)
Chasing God, Serving Man (Shippensburg, PA: Fresh Bread, 2001)

Amy Carmichael

Thou Givest...They Gather (Fort Washington, PA: Christian Literature Crusade, 1958)

Donald Durnbaugh

The Believer's Church (Ephrata, PA: Herald Press, 1968)

Phoebe Palmer

Entire Devotion to God (Salem, OH: Schmul Publishing, 1998)

Hannah More

The Religion of the Heart (Burlington, NJ; D. Allinson & Co., 1811)

A.W. Tozer

The Pursuit of God (Camp Hill, PA: Christian Publications, 1982)

Gems From Tozer (Camp Hill, PA: Christian Publications, 1979)

S.D. Gordon

Quiet Talks on Prayer
(www.poswords.org/articles/gordsd/prayer01.shtml)

Henry Drummond

Greatest Thing in the World
(www.ccel.org/d/drummond/greatest/greatest.txt)
Ideal Life (www.ccel.org)

Thetus Tenney

Prayer Takes Wings (Ventura, CA: Regal Books, 2000)

Leonard Ravenhill

Why Revival Tarries (Minneapolis, MN: Bethany, 1979)
Revival Praying (Minneapolis, MN: Bethany, 1981)

Thomas à Kempis

The Imitation of Christ (www.ccel.org)

Andrew Murray

With Christ in the School of Prayer (www.ccel.org)

Oswald Chambers

My Utmost for His Highest (www.ccel.org)

Madame Jeanne Guyon

Union With God (Jacksonville, FL; Christian Books Publishing House, 1999)

St. John of the Cross

Ascent of Mount Carmel (www.ccel.org)
Dark Night of the Soul (www.ccel.org)

Dietrich Bonhoeffer

The Cost of Discipleship (New York: Macmillan, 1959)

Bart Pierce

Seeking Our Brothers (Shippensburg, PA: Fresh Bread, 2000)

Dr. Marva Mitchell

It Takes a Church to Raise a Village (Shippensburg, PA: Treasure House, 2001)

Rich Marshall

God @ Work (Shippensburg, PA: Destiny Image, 2000)

Donald L. Milam, Jr.

The Lost Passions of Jesus (Shippensburg, PA: MercyPlace, 1999)

Howard Snyder

The Radical Wesley (Downers Grove, IL: InterVarsity Press, 1980)

Ministries Promoting Worship and Prayer

Intercessors International
P.O. Box 390
Bulverde, TX 78163

Friends of the Bridegroom
P.O. Box 35003
Kansas City, MO 64134

Wagner Leadership Institute
11005 Hwy 83 North
Colorado Springs, CO 80921

Missions Resources for Compassionate Service

American Bible Society
1865 Broadway
New York, NY 10023
www.biblesociety.org/bs-usa.htm

Ameritribes
P.O. Box 27346
Tucson, AZ 85726-7346
www.ameritribes.org

Campus Crusade for Christ International
100 Lake Hart Drive
Orlando, FL 32832
www.ccci.org

Christian and Missionary Alliance
P.O. Box 35000
Colorado Springs, CO 80935-3500
www.cmalliance.org

Christian Literature Crusade
701 Pennsylvania Ave.
Fort Washington, PA 19034
www.clcusa.org

European Christian Mission
110 Juanita Drive
South Zanesville, OH 43701
www.ecmi.org

Gospel for Asia
1932 Walnut Plaza
Carrollton, TX 75006
www.gfa.org

Gospel Missionary Union
10000 N Oak Trafficway
Kansas City, MO 64155
www.gmu.org

Gospel Recordings/Global Recordings Network
122 Glendale Blvd
Los Angles, CA 90026
www.gospelrecordings.com

Mission Aviation Fellowship
P.O. Box 3202
Redlands, CA 92374
www.maf.org

New Tribes Mission
1000 E First Street
Sanford, FL 32771
www.ntm.org

OMF International
10 W Dry Creek Circle
Littleton, CO 80120
www.omf.org

OMS International
941 Fry Road
Greenwood, IN 46142
www.omsinternational.org

Operation Mobilization, Inc.
P.O. Box 444
Tyrone, GA 30290
www.usa.om.org

Rainbows of Hope
P.O. Box 517
Fort Mill, SC 29716
www.wec-int.org/rainbows

SafeHouse Outreach
89 Ellis Street
Atlanta, GA 30303
www.SafeHouse-Outreach.org

TEAM (The Evangelical Alliance Mission)
P.O. Box 969
Wheaton, IL 60189
www.teamworld.org

United World Mission
P.O. Box 668767
Charlotte, NC 28270
www.uwm.org

WEC International
P.O. Box 1707
Fort Washington, PA 19034
www.wec-int.org

Wycliffe Bible Translators
P.O. Box 2727
Huntington Beach, CA 92647
www.wycliffe.org

Marketplace Resources for Faith at Work

National Center for Neighborhood Enterprise
1424 Sixteenth Street, NW
Washington, DC 20036

Lighthouse@Work
5666 Lincoln Dr.
Edina, MN 55436

Marketplace Ministries, Inc.
12900 Preston Rd. Ste 1215
Dallas, TX 75230

Full Gospel Business Men's Fellowship International
P.O. Box 19714
Irvine, CA 92623-9714

International Christian Chamber of Commerce
Hjälmarberget SE-70231
Örebro, Sweden

Marketplace Leaders
3520 Habersham Club Drive
Cumming, GA 30041

Faith At Work, Inc.
106 E Broad St #B
Falls Church, VA 22046-4501

The Avodah Institute
34 Chambers St.
Princeton, NJ 08542

Executive Ministries
201 West McBee Avenue, Ste 201
Greenville, SC 29601

American Center for Law and Justice
P.O. Box 64429
Virginia Beach, VA 23467

Fellowship of Companies for Christ International
4201 N. Peachtree Road, Ste 200
Atlanta, GA 30341

Workplace Wisdom Interactive
www.wowi.net

Ministries at Work on the Front Lines

Operation Blessing International
977 Centerville Turnpike
Virginia Beach, VA 23463

Teen Challenge International
3728 W. Chestnut Expy
Springfield, MO 65802

World Vision Inc.
P.O. Box 9716
Federal Way, WA 98063-9716

We Care America, Inc.
702 Boulevard, SE
Atlanta, GA 30312

Compassion International
Colorado Springs, CO 80997

Mission America Lighthouse Movement
P.O. Box 13930
Palm Desert, CA 92255

Blood n Fire
188 Martin Luther King Drive SE,
Atlanta, GA 30312

Prison Fellowship Ministries
P.O. Box 1550
Merrifield, VA 22116-1550

Convoy of Hope
330 S. Patterson Ave.
Springfield, MO 65802

Dream Center International
2301 Bellevue Avenue
Los Angeles, CA 90026

Global Compassion Network
1607 Cromwell Bridge Road
Baltimore, MD 21234

Harvest Evangelism, Inc.
6472 Camden Avenue, Ste. 110
San Jose, CA 95120

March for Jesus USA
P.O. Box 6884
Atlanta, GA 30315

Somebody Cares
PO Box 925308
Houston, TX 77292-5308

Victory Christian Center
7700 South Lewis Avenue
Tulsa, OK 74136-7700

World Relief
PO Box 597
Baltimore, MD 21203

Mercy Ships International
P.O. Box 2020
Garden Valley, TX 75771-2020

Teen Mania
P.O. Box 2000
Garden Valley, TX 75771

Youth With A Mission
7085 Battlecreek Road SE
Salem, OR 97301

Internet Resources

www.ccel.org

www.dreamcenter.org/

www.ob.org

www.mercyships.com/sitemap.shtml

www.christianity.com/prisonfellowship

www.worldvision.org

www.wecareamerica.org

www.teenchallenge.com

www.convoyofhope.org

www.lighthousemovement.com

www.fgbmfi.org

www.marketplaceministries.com

www.iccc.net

www.marketplaceleaders.org/

www.ywam.org/

www.teenmania.com

www.revival-library.org

GodChasers.network is the ministry of Tommy and Jean-
nie Tenney. Their heart's desire is to see the presence and
power of God fall—not just in churches, but on cities and
communities all over the world.

How to contact us:

By Mail:

GodChasers.network
P.O. Box 3355
Pineville, Louisiana 71361
USA

By Phone:

Voice: 318.44CHASE (318.442.4273)
Fax: 318.442.6884
Orders: 888.433.3355

By Internet:

E-mail: GodChaser@GodChasers.net
Website: www.GodChasers.net

 # Join Today

When you join the **GodChasers.network** we'll send you a free teaching tape!

If you share in our vision and want to stay current on how the Lord is using GodChasers.network, please add your name to our mailing list. We'd like to keep you updated on what the Spirit is saying through Tommy. We'll also send schedule updates and make you aware of new resources as they become available.

Sign up by calling or writing to:

Tommy Tenney
GodChasers.network
P.O. Box 3355
Pineville, Louisiana 71361-3355
USA

318-44CHASE (318.442.4273)
or sign up online at http://www.GodChasers.net/lists/

We regret that we are only able to send regular postal mailings to certain countries at this time. If you live outside the U.S. you can still add your postal address to our mailing list—you will automatically begin to receive our mailings as soon as they are available in your area.

E-mail Announcement List

If you'd like to receive information from us via e-mail, just provide an e-mail address when you contact us and let us know that you want to be included on the e-mail announcement list!

BOOKS BY

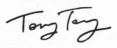

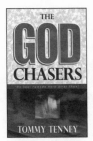

THE GOD CHASERS

$12.00 plus $4.50 S&H

What is a God Chaser? A person whose hunger exceeds his reach...a person whose passion for God's presence presses him to chase the impossible in hopes that the uncatchable might catch him.

The great GodChasers of the Scripture—Moses, Daniel, David—see how they were driven by hunger born of tasting His goodness. They had seen the invisible and nothing else satisfied. Add your name to the list. Come join the ranks of the God Chasers.

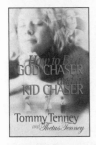

CHASING GOD, SERVING MAN

$17.00 plus $4.50 S&H

Using the backdrop of Bethany and the house of Mary and Martha, Tommy Tenney biblically explores new territory. The revolutionary concepts in this book can change your life. You will discover who you really are (and unlock the secret of who "they" really are)!

HOW TO BE A GOD CHASER AND A KID CHASER

$12.00 plus $4.50 S&H

Combining years of both spiritual passion and practical parenting, Tommy Tenney and his mother, Thetus Tenney, answer the questions that every parent has. Helping them are the touching and sometimes humorous insights of such Christian greats as Dutch and Ceci Sheets, Cindy Jacobs and others. You'll have to open this book to discover.

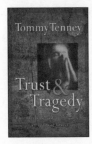

TRUST AND TRAGEDY

$7.00 plus $4.50 S&H

When tragedy strikes, your desperate hunt for hope in the secular forest will be futile. The hunters invariably go home emptyhanded and brokenhearted, because humanity doesn't have the answers. Jesus gave us the key in one of the most direct and unequivocal statements ever made: "I am the way, the truth, and the life. No one comes to the Father, except through me." This book is a signpost along the way, through the truth, and to the life. If life is what you need, trust in God will take you there.

GodChasers.network
P.O. Box 3355, Pineville, Louisiana 71361-3355
318-44CHASE (318.442.4273)
www.GodChasers.net

VIDEOTAPE ALBUMS BY

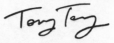

GOING HOME FROM A FUNERAL
Video $20.00 $10.00 plus $4.50 S&H

Our country is now in a crisis. Some things will never be the same. Our national mentality is as if we are "going home from a funeral." We are no longer in the orderly, controlled funeral procession. Cars have scattered, taking their own routes back to individual homes and routines. The lights are off and reality hits.

FOLLOW THE MAN ON THE COLT
Video $20.00 plus $4.50 S&H

From humility to authority.... If we learn to ride the colt of humility, then we qualify to ride on the stallion of authority.

(This new video helps us understand that we all start this journey crawling—which strenghthens us to walk—that empowers us to run—and rewards us to ride!) Enjoy this great teaching by Tommy Tenney on following the Man on the colt. It will change the way you see the obstacles put in your path! Remember, there is never a testimony without a test!

BROWNSVILLE WILDFIRE SERIES, VOL. 1
"Born to Be a Worshiper"
Video $20.00 plus $4.50 S&H

God would rather hear the passionate praises of His children than the perfection of heavenly worship. It isn't about how good we are as singers, or how skilled we are as musicians. It isn't about singing catchy choruses with clever words. It's all about GOD, and if we'll let our guard down and allow ourselves to truly worship Him, we'll find that He's closer than we ever imagined. If you've been born into God's kingdom, then you were born to be a worshiper! It's time to do the very thing that we were created for!

TURNING ON THE LIGHT OF THE GLORY
Video $20.00 plus $4.50 S&H

Tommy deals with turning on the light of the glory and presence of God, and he walks us through the necessary process and ingredients to potentially unleash what His Body has always dreamed of.

GodChasers.network
P.O. Box 3355, Pineville, Louisiana 71361-3355
318-44CHASE (318.442.4273)
www.GodChasers.net

AUDIOTAPE ALBUMS BY

Tommy Tenney

WHAT'S THE FIGHT ABOUT?
(audiotape album) $20 plus $4.50 S&H

Tape 1 — Preserving the Family: God's special gift to the world is the family! If we don't preserve the family, the church is one generation from extinction. God's desire is to heal the wounds of the family from the inside out.

Tape 2 — Unity in the Body: An examination of the levels of unity that must be respected and achieved before "Father let them be one" becomes an answered prayer!

Tape 3 — "IF you're throwing dirt, you're just losing ground!" In "What's the Fight About?" Tommy invades our backyards to help us discover our differences are not so different after all!

FANNING THE FLAMES
(audiotape album) $20 plus $4.50 S&H

Tape 1 — The Application of the Blood and the Ark of the Covenant: Most of the churches in America today dwell in an outer-court experience. Jesus made atonement with His own blood, once and for all, and the veil in the temple was rent from top to bottom.

Tape 2 — A Tale of Two Cities—Nazareth & Nineveh: What city is more likely to experience revival: Nazareth or Nineveh? You might be surprised....

Tape 3 — The "I" Factor: Examine the difference between *ikabod* and *kabod* ("glory"). The arm of flesh cannot achieve what needs to be done. God doesn't need us; we need Him.

KEYS TO LIVING THE REVIVED LIFE
(audiotape album) $20 plus $4.50 S&H

Tape 1 — Fear Not: To have no fear is to have faith, and perfect love casts out fear, so we must establish the trust of a child in our loving Father.

Tape 2 — Hanging in There: Have you ever been tempted to give up, quit, and throw in the towel? This message is a word of encouragement for you.

Tape 3 — Fire of God: Fire purges the sewer of our souls and destroys the hidden things that would cause disease. Learn the way out of a repetitive cycle of seasonal times of failure.

PURSUING HIS PRESENCE
(audiotape album) $20 plus $4.50 S&H

Tape 1 — Transporting the Glory: There comes a time when God wants us to grow to another level of maturity. For us, that means walking by the Spirit rather than according to the flesh.

Tape 2 — Turning on the Light of the Glory: Tommy walks us through the process of unleashing what the Body of Christ has always dreamed of: getting to the Glory!

Tape 3 — Building a Mercy Seat: In worship, we create an appropriate environment in which the presence of God can dwell. The focus of the church needs to be shifted from simply dusting the furniture to building the mercy seat.

GodChasers.network
P.O. Box 3355, Pineville, Louisiana 71361-3355
318-44CHASE (318.442.4273)
www.GodChasers.net

Run With Us!

Become a GodChasers.network Monthly Revival Partner

Two men, a farmer and his friend, were looking out over the farmer's fields one afternoon. It was a beautiful sight—it was nearly harvest time, and the wheat was swaying gently in the wind. Inspired by this idyllic scene, the friend said, "Look at God's provision!" The farmer replied, "You should have seen it when God had it by Himself!"

This humorous story illustrates a serious truth. Every good and perfect gift comes from Him: but we are supposed to be more than just passive recipients of His grace and blessings. We must never forget that only God can cause a plant to grow—but it is equally important to remember that *we are called to do our part in the sowing, watering, and harvesting.*

When you sow seed into this ministry, you help us reach people and places you could never imagine. The faithful support of individuals like you allows us to send resources, free of charge, to many who would otherwise be unable to obtain them. Your gifts help us carry the gospel all over the world—including countries that have been closed to evangelism. Would you prayerfully consider partnering with us? As a small token of our gratitude, our Revival Partners who send a monthly gift of $30 or more receive a teaching tape every month. This ministry could not survive without the faithful support of partners like you!

Stand with me now—so we can run together later!

In Pursuit,

Tommy Tenney

Tommy Tenney

**Become a Monthly Revival Partner
by calling or writing to:**

Tommy Tenney/GodChasers.network
**P.O. Box 3355
Pineville, Louisiana 71361-3355
318.44CHASE (318.442.4273)**